Christmas on crack

Edited by
Carlton Mellick III

Eraserhead Press
Portland, OR

ERASERHEAD PRESS
205 NE BRYANT
PORTLAND, OR 97211

WWW.ERASERHEADPRESS.COM

ISBN: 1-936383-38-1

Copyright © 2010 by Carlton Mellick III, Jordan Krall, Jeff Burk, Andrew Goldfarb, Kevin L. Donihe, Edmund Colell, Cameron Pierce, Kirsten Alene, and Kevin Shamel.

Interior art copyright © 2010 by Andrew Goldfarb

Cover art copyright © 2010 by Ed Mironiuk
http://www.edmironiuk.com

All rights reserved. No part of this book may be reproduced or transmitted in any form or by any means, electronic or mechanical, including photocopying, recording, or by any information storage and retrieval system, without the written consent of the publisher, except where permitted by law.

Printed in the USA.

TABLE OF CONTENTS

EDITOR'S NOTE by Carlton Mellick III ... 5

SANTA CLAUS AND THE ELVES OF FUCK
JORDAN KRALL
7

FROSTY AND THE FULL MONTY
JEFF BURK
53

UNWANTED GIFTS
ANDREW GOLDFARB
62

TWO-WAY SANTA
KEVIN L. DONIHE
63

THE CHRISTMAS TURN-ON
EDMUND COLELL
77

THE ELF SLUT SISTERS
CAMERON PIERCE & KIRSTEN ALENE
95

CHRISTMAS CRABS
KEVIN SHAMEL
117

EDITOR'S NOTE

For some, Christmas is a time of family bonding, Christianity, and awesome fucking toys. But for me, it is a little more special than that. I view Christmas as the time of peppermint dominatrixes, elf orgies, snowjobs, and getting drunk with fat guys. So I have decided to share with you my true meaning of Christmas with this book, *Christmas on Crack*, a collection of magical holiday tales written by members of my family: the bizarro fiction community. Besides releasing this as a companion piece to my own Christmas book, Sausagey Santa, I've also released it as a way to introduce my readers to other writers in the bizarro fiction scene. So read these tales and if you like them check out some of the authors' books. Underground writers could use your support.

So, I hope you enjoy these Christmas tales of bizarro debauchery. Consider it my Christmas present to you. If you're good I might give you another Christmas present next year. But if you're bad, I guess you're kind of fucked, because Creepy Cowboy Santa (pictured left) likes to hang naughty boys and girls . . . Not to kill you or anything, he just hangs you for a few minutes because he's got a strangling fetish. He might even pay you if you let him do it, and that's pretty cool. A little extra money around Christmas is always good. It's a win-win situation.

Merry Christmas and shit,
- Carlton Mellick III 12/01/10

SANTA CLAUS

and

the ELVES of FUCK

BY

Jordan Krall

Jordan Krall *is one of my favorite writers in the bizarro fiction scene. He's got a way of writing that is completely addicting to me, especially if you read a few of his works in a row. I recommend picking up his books* Squid Pulp Blues *and* Piecemeal June. *By the end of them you'll be rushing out to get his crazy spaghetti western,* Fistful of Feet, *and then wishing he could write books faster. Because Jordan's work is always filled with characters who have crazy fetishes, I knew he would be perfect for this book. In fact, if I couldn't get Jordan I wasn't planning on doing* Christmas on Crack *at all. This book was made for him.*

So get cozy around the crackling fireplace and enjoy this tale of Santa's encounter with Ms. Peppermint. It will surely send visions of sugar plums dancing through your head . . .

I.

Christmas.
What a pain in my ass!
Santa Claus picked a flea out of his beard and flicked it into the sky. He pulled on the reins, cursing those fucking reindeer for not going fast enough, for not ending his hell sooner. Once a year he had to endure the most ridiculous of responsibilities which was to provide toys to the children of the world.

Santa wouldn't have much of a problem with Christmas if he just had to deliver to poor kids or orphans. But no, much of his time was devoted to delivering to rich, spoiled brats whose parents gave them everything they wanted anyway. That was the worst. Those were the times when he was tempted to take a big old shit in their stockings. It took every ounce of his jolly spirit to resist the urge. He had to tell himself it was only once a year, but even that wasn't enough to extinguish the hate that engulfed him.

And shit, this year was just too much for him. His back was sore, his stomach upset, and his dick, well, his dick was desperate for some action. Mrs. Claus hadn't given it up for months, not since she caught Santa with that Russian whore.

That was a bad fuckin' night.
Santa had ordered the girl from Russia with the intention of just getting a quick screw to satisfy his need for variety. Wasn't it normal for any man to want to dig into

some strange pussy every once in a while? It wasn't that he didn't love his wife but he had to be honest about it. After three hundred and fifty years of marriage, the young and beautiful Mrs. Diana Claus just wasn't giving the same effort in the bedroom as she had in the beginning.

So last year Santa had forgotten to lock his workshop door and Mrs. Claus had caught him squeezing his jolly red penis into a tight Russian clamhole. If it wasn't for the poor hooker bursting into tears, there would've been a double homicide. Mrs. Claus was furious to the point of putting a blowtorch to her husband's crotch and threatening to burn his pecker off if he didn't repent right then and there.

Fortunately, Santa dropped to his knees and repented.

He also agreed to send the Russian girl back to her home country, but the girl begged and pleaded for him to send her anywhere but there. She said if her uncles found out she didn't fulfill her part of the transaction, they'd lock her in that toxic waste barrel again. She couldn't stand another week in there. It had made her brain bubble.

Despite her own emotional turmoil, Mrs. Claus agreed to instead send the young Russian girl to New Jersey where she could get a job as a stripper. After all, it hadn't been the girl's fault that Santa Claus was such a letch.

Santa had promised his wife he'd never do that sort of thing again and he meant it. But after a few weeks, that didn't satisfy her. She kept hounding him to explain why he'd pick some young Russian whore when he had such a hot, young wife at home. Santa didn't really have a reason. He admitted it seemed strange, since most men would kill to have a young wife like Diana at home. She had cute, perky breasts and a petite body that would bring any cock to attention. But the Russian girl he brought over was plump and voluptuous like a juicy sugarplum. Yes, it was true Santa was one of the most magical men in the world, but he was still a *man*.

He had promised Diana that he wouldn't stray again and had intended to keep that promise. But couldn't she at least give him an occasional handjob or something? Instead, she neglected the intimate part of their marriage and expected him to satisfy himself *alone*. The whole fucking thing was just too damn frustrating and on top of that, he had to deliver fucking toys again.

Let's get this shit over with.

Santa shook his head free from stress and looked down at the last stop on his Christmas delivery route. It was a new town that had just popped up out of nowhere. There didn't appear to be any industry nearby, no coal mines or anything like that. It was as if a group of people just decided to settle themselves on a plot of land like their ancestors would have done hundreds of years ago.

It was situated between two snowy mountains, cradled like a nursery filled with brick and wood babies. Santa thought the place looked like a shit-hole but it possessed a weird, quaint sort of charm that wasn't usually evident in new towns. If he didn't know better, Santa would have guessed the town was at least three hundred years old.

But Santa really didn't give a shit about the specifics of the place. He automatically resented it and its residents for providing him with an additional delivery stop. He couldn't wait to get home and kick back with a drink. That would be the routine for the next eleven months. Twelve hours a day of watching kung-fu movies while drinking rum and donkey's milk. That is, until next December rolled around and he'd have to start preparing for the holidays.

"Okay, you rat bastards, bring me on down," Santa said to the reindeer. "Let's dump our shit and get the hell out of here."

The animals answered by snorting and dropping straight down through the air, forcing Santa back in his seat. "Okay, okay, not so fast!" he said, pulling the reins until they cut into his hands and drew blood. "Shit!"

Deep red blood leaked onto the sleigh and formed the shape of a pair of high heels. Santa looked down at it and smudged it with his elbow as the reindeer pulled the vehicle down closer and closer to the town.

As the sleigh reached the rooftops, Santa saw a decorative wooden sign, lit up by multi-colored Christmas lights:

WELCOME TO TUSK
Population 2,976
"A little town...just for you...."

"Yeah, yeah, kiss my ass," Santa said, as he landed the sleigh on the first house.

II.

Diana Claus sat on her front porch and looked out at the North Pole, her village of Christmas Spirit, her kingdom of holiday cheer, her dominion of toys and joy.

"Son of a bitch," she said.

She knew that it was her husband's job to be out all night delivering toys but she couldn't shake the feeling that he'd use the opportunity to screw around behind her back. Despite his tight schedule, Diana knew he'd find a way to squeeze in a blowjob or a quick fuck somewhere, probably Amsterdam or Newark. He'd probably hire some slut to dress up like that one-eyed woman from that movie he liked so much, the one where the bad-ass chick gets revenge. The eye patch really made Santa's dick hard but Diana refused to wear one. It was just plain weird. But that probably meant some other bitch was wearing one for him.

Well, fuck it.

She had it. She was sick of being humiliated. Sure, he'd promised he'd never cheat on her again but could she believe him? He was a man, after all. Diana was considerably younger than he was, still had her figure, and had not a wrinkle on her face. Yet he still found the need to order himself a chubby Russian girl!

The rage and resentment had been building inside her ever since "the incident" and it had boiled over into a plan.

It was a plan that involved sacrificing her lifestyle or at least temporarily altering it. That is, *if* they could be settled. The plan would have to be executed with meticulous skill, but Diana didn't feel like she had the patience to do it herself.

That's why she called *them*.

The Elves of Fuck.

Contrary to popular belief, Christmas elves weren't the only kind of elves around. In fact, they were a small minority among the elf race. There were dozens of varieties of elves and Mrs. Claus counted on the rumors being true, that the Elves of Fuck were the ones to call when you needed something done about an unfaithful spouse.

Apparently they also had their tiny hands in the pornography business, producing fetish films for customers who found midgets to be a bit too disproportionate. Diana had actually found out about them after viewing one of their films, *Spit Shine My Face #4*, which consisted of five elf women spitting on and slapping a regular-sized man. It hadn't been her cup of tea but she was thankful that it introduced her to the Elves of Fuck.

So there she was, sitting on her front porch on Christmas Eve, waiting for her elf contact to come along and give her an update. A part of her hoped that her fears would be unfounded and Santa would not be sniffing around strange snatch. Maybe then they could repair their marriage and she could go back to trusting him wholeheartedly like she had done in the beginning.

From behind her, a voice said, "Diana?"

She turned and saw that it was Smitty, her squidfoot.

Smitty had been found roaming the North Pole ten years prior. At first, Diana was terrified of him. After all, he was seven-feet tall and hairy, looking like a cross between a sasquatch and a squid. After spending some time with him, however, Diana learned that he wasn't the monstrous beast she had expected. In fact, Smitty was quite gentle and cultured.

"Hey there!" she said.

Smitty said, "So you're really going through with it, Diana?"

"Yeah. Why? You don't think I should?"

"I'm just saying, you open up this can of worms and who knows what kind of repercussions will come squirming out. Those elves mean business, you know."

"I know. That's why I hired them."

"Did you speak to them already?"

"Yeah. Someone should be here any minute. I told them not to do anything until I say so."

Smitty put a tentacle on Diana's shoulder. "And what if they tell you he's messing around with someone else?"

"Then I tell them to kill the son of a bitch."

Smitty sighed. "Spoken like a true wife."

"Hey, I've given him more than enough opportunities to show me that he truly wants to be faithful and if he's not messing around, he has nothing to worry about. If he is, then he deserves it."

"But what about all the kids? What about Christmas?"

"Oh, fuck Christmas. If no one is able to take over the job, then all those whiny brats don't get their stupid little toys."

Before Smitty could respond, a flash of light appeared in front of them. The flash morphed into a cloud of purple smoke and out of that smoke walked an elf. A naked elf.

III.

Santa had delivered to three houses when he realized something was strange about the town.

The three houses he had delivered in didn't seem right. The living rooms felt phony, as if they were all sets from a movie or television show. Sure, there were signs of habitation (framed pictures, children's toys spread across the floor, food in the fridge) but there was an emptiness that could only be felt and not seen. Santa was tempted to look into the rooms so he could see for himself that there were people living there, but he resisted the urge. Doing something like that could only bring trouble.

It was while sneaking around the back of the fourth house that he smelled the peppermint.

Santa sniffed and realized that it wasn't just peppermint. There was a musky odor in there and a fishy smell that was not entirely unpleasant.

He was about to try to follow the smell when, from behind him, there was the sound of giggling.

"Yoohoo," a woman's voice purred. "Oh my, oh my, oh my. Is it true?"

Santa put his hand to his forehead. *Awww, shit.*

This had happened two years before. Santa had been caught by some nosey good-for-nothing teenage boy over in Dayton, Ohio. It had resulted in his having to commit his first and only kidnapping. He felt slightly guilty for having to drop the fucker into a volcano on the sleigh ride back to the North Pole but it had to be done.

Still, he didn't want to have to do it again.

He turned around but didn't see the woman. She was in the shadows. He said, "Shhhhhhhh…Be quiet. You're dreaming." It was a lame trick that rarely worked but he had to try it.

"No need to be quiet, sweetie, oh, sweetie," she said. "I know who you are, I do. See?" She stepped out of the snowy shadows.

Santa nearly fell over. The woman that stood before him was the most beautiful he had ever seen. If he had believed in angels, he'd have sworn she was one.

She seemed ageless, though if Santa had to guess, he'd say she was probably forty, maybe forty-five years old. Even so, every one of those years must have been smooth ones. Even the small wrinkles on her face looked as if drawn by a god.

Her breasts were massive, bulging forward, struggling against her dark red business suit. Santa's eyes moved downward and saw she wore high heels, glittery red like

Dorothy's shoes in The Wizard of Oz. Santa thought that was funny. Sexy, but funny. He imagined those shoes clicking together, summoning the Lollipop Guild but instead of munchkins, they'd be elves whose sole purpose was to give those shoes (and the feet within) a tongue bath.

His eyes went back to her breasts. "Uh," was all he could manage to say.

"No words?" she said. "You're looking at my chest. Have anything to get off yours?"

The peppermint scent grew stronger, forcing itself up Santa's nostrils and into his head until he felt like his brain was aflame with mint fire. He kept staring at the woman, from her wiggling toes trapped in her glittery shoes up to her thick thighs that were barely covered by her tight skirt. What was she doing out in the snow dressed like that? She didn't even have a coat on. But he wasn't complaining. If she had worn a coat, he would never have gotten such a good look at her....

"Chest?" he said.

The woman took a step closer. "Yes. Do you have anything to get off your chest? Such as who you really are. You're not some shopping mall Santa Claus, are you? You're the real deal, the real McCoy, the whole kit and caboodle. Saint Nicolas himself, not some butter-and-egg man coming through the humble little town of Tusk."

"I, uh, don't know what you're...." he said. Before he could finish, however, Santa realized he was an inch away from the woman, eye-level with her cleavage as it spoke to him like erotic hieroglyphs. Snowflakes were falling between her breasts, moistening them. Santa imagined the woman drooling onto her own cleavage, making it sloppy for him to bury his face in. A snow and saliva ride through her plump, milky valley.

She said, "Oh, silly man, I know all about you. I know your real name isn't Nicolas but I do know you're a saint. Well, you used to be, anyway. So sad to hear what happened."

Still staring at the hypnotic cleavage, Santa Claus tried shaking himself out of whatever witchcraft the woman had him trapped in. How did she know who he really was? How did she know what had happened to him all those years ago? There were perhaps five people, maybe six, who knew about his losing his sainthood back in '23.

The woman shook her chest. "It was nice of the council to let you keep your job, you know, after everything."

"Who are you?" he said. "Do I know you?"

Santa felt the tip of his nose touch her chest. He smelled peppermint, sweat, and…what was that? Talcum powder?

She giggled, flashing her tiny white teeth. "Know me? Oh, silly, of course not. Why would you know little old me? I'm just a boring girl from a boring town." She leaned in close, nearly smothering Santa between her breasts.

As he spoke, Santa felt his lips tingle against the woman's skin. "What are you doing to me?"

"Oh, silly. *I'm* not doing anything to *you*," she said, as she grabbed the back of Santa's head and pushed it down to her crotch.

IV.

"Mrs. Claus," the naked elf said. "My name is Aleph. I believe you spoke to my associate, Gimel."

Diana stood up and offered Aleph her hand. "Hi, nice to meet you. Yes, I talked to Gimel this morning about my husband."

Aleph shook her hand quickly. He looked at Smitty and then back at Diana. "Before we get down to business, are you available to speak now? What I mean to say is, I'm not at liberty to speak about this in front of anyone but you."

"Oh, yes well, Smitty was just leaving," she said. She smiled at the squidfoot. "I'll talk to you later, hon, okay?"

Smitty nodded and walked into the street, sliding across the snow on his tentacle-feet.

Diana said, "So, yes, I talked to Gimel this morning."

"Yes, unfortunately he wasn't able to meet with you personally. Being his supervisor, I'll brief you on the current situation." Aleph pointed to a chair. "May I?"

"Of course." Diana motioned with her hand for him to sit. When he did, she noticed that, despite his having a rather long penis, he lacked a scrotum.

Aleph handed her a folder and said, "Though our organization is known for solving these sorts of…problems, we really get no pleasure in relaying this information. It's simply a job that needs to be done and we are willing to do it. I know it's a rather difficult thing to deal with, being a spouse of—"

Diana said, "I don't need the 'poor wife' speech. Just tell me what you have to tell me."

Aleph sighed. He opened a folder that appeared out of thin air. "Okay. Here's where we're at…."

V.

Santa Claus felt like crabmeat squeezed into a sweaty leather glove. There was something coming out of the darkness. There were….

Sugarplums.

Sugarplums covered in vulgar snail shells spinning on axe blades. Sugarplums rolling like dice across the pudding-covered floor. Sugarplums giving birth to Saturn's rings spinning out of control, spinning into other sugarplums made of hairy flaps of pink meat. Sugarplums with legs running to other sugarplums with arms, colliding to form Siamese chunks of quivering fruit-flesh. Sugarplum snowflakes falling like unlucky jumpers from skyscrapers that burn like Yule logs.

What the hell is happening?

Santa closed his eyes, saw starbursts and tasted copper. He tried spitting out the mouthful of liquid pennies but couldn't do it.

He opened his eyes. The sugarplums were still there. Some of them now wore wooden masks while others were covered in sheep skin and goat horns. Those fucking sugarplums were going to drive him insane.

How'd I get here?

Oh yeah, that woman. That beautiful woman. The angel. Oh my god, those tits, I remember those tits. Where the hell is she? Those sugarplums sorta look like tits. Angelic tits ready to burst...a milky supernova...all over my face....

Santa felt a hand on the back of his head and he was shoved straight into the sheep skin sugarplums, which were now twisting into tentacles of red meat.

A voice reverberated through the void. "Eat...."

And Santa started to eat.

VI.

Diana Claus closed the folder full of photographs. She lifted a hand to her forehead and then ran it through her hair. "I can't believe that bastard. After all the promises, all that shit."

Aleph nodded but did not reply even though he knew that Mrs. Claus expected him to. But he hadn't been hired to be a marriage counselor.

She said, "Who is she? Another Russian slut?"

"No, she is not. Who she is exactly, well, we have not been able to confirm anything. As far as we know, she is just a woman from town, from your husband's last stop, I mean."

Diana turned her head and looked at the family photos hanging on the wall. "Well, I want it to be his last stop for good. You do know what I'm talking about, right?"

Aleph nodded. "I do."

"So you'll do it," she said.

"I will but only if that's what you really want. I'll meet with my team, discuss the consequences of that action and we will bring it to you in writing. If you still would like to go through with hiring us for that additional task, we will do the job and do it well."

Diana nodded.

"Then I'll be back in a half hour with the paperwork."

"Okay."

Aleph stood up and started for the door. He stopped. "One more thing."

"Yes?"

"This woman, she acted like she knew your husband even though he seemed to have no idea. Does she look familiar to you?"

Diana reluctantly opened the folder again and perused the photographs. "No, I don't think I've ever seen her before."

Aleph frowned and continued on his way out of the room.

VII.

Santa's mouth burned. His lips, his tongue, hell, even his teeth felt like they were on fire. What the hell did she do to him? All he could remember was being shoved down face-first into her crotch, forced to suck and lick his way through three hours of warm, wet suffocation. He had only the slightest recollection of something else.

Sugarplums?

There was a flood of musky peppermint goo that left him gagging and gasping.

He looked around but saw nothing in the darkness. It was cold but dry so he wasn't out in the snow. Was he in a bed? Santa moved his arms around, hoping to feel expensive Egyptian cotton, but instead found himself engulfed in what felt like taffy.

What the hell is going on?

Though he had ceased to believe in the god of his fathers, Santa thought maybe the woman was some sort of avenging angel that had come down to punish him for his past infidelities. But that didn't make sense. Would an angel force a sinner to pleasure her?

Maybe. Santa hated having to speculate. He valued simplicity and hated when shit got complicated.

A clip-clop sound echoed around him. The sound was familiar.

What is that?

Santa racked his brain trying to identify the sound. First he thought it might be the reins of the reindeer but that was more of a slap-slap sound, not a clip-clop. Then he thought it might be horse hooves but that didn't seem right. As the clip-clop sound got louder and louder, he finally identified it.

High heels.

The clip-clop sound ceased and was followed by a click. Bright lights shocked Santa and he found himself looking at the woman's hips, tightly hugged by her business suit.

"What did you do to me?" he said.

The woman crouched down so she was face to face with him. "I made you eat my pussy. Is your memory that bad?"

Santa shook his head and looked around. He was lying on a bed made of a dark red substance that did resemble the taffy it felt like. It didn't look edible, though. There was an odd metallic look to it as if it were robot puke. "Why?" he said.

She laughed. "Why did I make you eat my pussy? Oh my, that's a simple question. It's because I wanted my pussy eaten. I wanted to have an orgasm. What other reason would there be? You think maybe I thought the Easter Bunny lived inside my twat and wanted you to speak to him?"

"Who are you?" Santa said, intentionally ignoring her question. If he was going to get some answers, he had to be stern.

"Well, that's a tough one, dear oh dear, as people call me different things depending on........." She rolled her eyes. "Well, whatever. You can call me Kay."

When Santa had asked the question, he hadn't really wanted to know her name as much as what the fuck she was doing to him. "What now?"

Kay laughed. "You want to leave, dearie? Really? Just think about that. Examine your feelings for five minutes and then I'll come back and you tell me if you really want to leave. Okay?"

With more clip-clopping, Kay left the room, shutting

the lights off as she did. Santa was left in the dark again. This time, however, he had something to think about. Did he really consider his situation a negative one? After all, he wasn't looking forward to finishing his Christmas route. This was a perfect excuse. He'd been fucking *abducted*. Who could blame him for not delivering the last batch of toys?

But was it really a kidnapping if he was being given the choice to leave?

Anyway, his wife wouldn't understand. She'd probably think he staged the whole thing just to get laid.

But there was one big problem. Despite her beauty, sex appeal, and those glorious, glorious breasts, this Kay woman seemed dangerous. Santa wasn't going to trust that she wasn't going to hurt him. Magnificent cleavage aside, she could very well be the death of him.

His lips were still burning from Kay's peppermint snatch juice and he wondered if it had been poisoned. Maybe that was the plan. She'd let him take five minutes to think about staying while the poison coursed through his body, getting him closer and closer to death by cunnilingus.

Santa decided he'd take his chances with Kay. He still loved his wife Diana but he just couldn't see himself walking away from this new woman without experiencing something worse.

If that meant Diana divorcing him, then he'd have to take that chance.

VIII.

Aleph nodded to the elf in front of him and then said, "Anything new?"

"After observing the subject following a woman to her

house, which you have pictures of, he proceeded to perform oral sex on her," Simon said. He was nervous because Aleph was the top guy in the unit and was talking directly to him. "We have a video link up so we'll be able to show the subject's wife."

"Okay, good," Aleph said. "But let's cut the shit. You can call him Mr. Claus and his wife Mrs. Claus. Sometimes the professionalism wears a little thin."

"Yes sir."

"Mrs. Claus is leaning towards termination of her husband so once she signs the papers, it's a go."

"Did she say how she wanted it done?"

Aleph shook his head. "No, but in most cases, the wives don't usually bring that up. I'll give her a few choices. I imagine she'll probably just tell me to make it quick, but to also let him know why it's happening."

"And the mystery woman?"

"I have to think about that. There's something strange about her and I'd like to investigate further before we do anything rash. But if she gets in the way, I will not hesitate to give the order for termination. We can't afford another slip-up like last year."

Simon gulped. "You mean St. Petersburg?"

"Yeah," Aleph said. "If that happens again, we're all fucked. You'll be fired and I'll be licking the pecker snot off the floor of the Yuletide whorehouses. I'm not doing that." Aleph turned and started to the door. "Never again."

IX.

Santa woke up and realized that he had been moved out of the taffy bed.

He was now lying on his back, his head enclosed in a wooden box. There was a round hole on top covered with black silk. The whole thing sort of looked familiar to him. What did it remind him of?

Oh yeah. A toilet.

He tried moving his arms and legs but found them dead. *I'm trapped in a fucking toilet.*

Through the wooden box, he heard the clip-clop of Kay's high heels. Here she comes again, coming to continue her sexy torture.

Clip-Clop. Clip-Clop.

She was getting closer.

CLIP-clop.

She was only a few feet of way.

CLIP-CLOP. CLIP-CLOP.

Then another sound: Kay clearing her throat.

Santa squinted when the black silk was moved. Through the squinting, Kay's face appeared above the hole, like an angel framed by a halo. His eyes moved to her stunning cleavage.

Then Kay smirked, cleared her throat a little more, and then spat on his face. The gob of phlegm splattered against his nose, clogging his nostrils.

"Rise and shine, honey bunch," she said. "I hope you appreciate my morning throat-jelly." Kay cleared her throat again and spat onto Santa's lips. "Taste good?"

Santa tried moving his face to get the mess off him but to no avail.

Kay said, "I know you're probably worried about not being able to move your arms and legs and I'm real sorry I had to do that. It's temporary or at least it should be. I used some venom I took out of the black belly of a tarantula and it's usually pretty harmless in the long run. Usually."

Santa felt weird talking to her while his head was trapped in the wooden box but he said, "Where am I? What are you doing to me?" Her loogie dripped from his lips into his mouth and Santa swallowed reluctantly. It tasted like gooey mint-flavored jam.

"The answer to your first question, well, you're in my bitch-box. I suppose your next question would be 'what's a bitch-box?' so I guess I'll answer that one, too. A bitch-box is a box where I keep my bitches. And you're my bitch now. And to answer your other question, about what I'm going to do to you...I'll let you figure that one out. I'll just have a seat while you think about it."

And with that, Kay moved her face away from the hole and stood up. She pulled up her skirt, pulled down her pantyhose, and placed her pale, plump ass onto the hole, blocking out the light and giving Santa an intimate view of her anus.

Goddamn, you're kidding me, right?

He stared at her brown pucker, hoping to somehow get her off the box using only his willpower.

But then her anus winked at him.

"Time's up," Kay said.

Santa's throat constricted. He closed his eyes.

Oh no. No. No. No.

X.

It only took Aleph a half hour to give Mrs. Claus the paperwork. She had been surprised how fast they worked but then she remembered the elves had the ability to teleport or something.

After only five minutes of reading through the details, Diana decided to go through with having her husband killed. If the proposed timeline Aleph gave her was to be believed, Santa Claus would be dead within the hour.

"You're sure?" Aleph said.

"Yes."

"If you look at page thirteen, you'll see the choices of termination."

Diana flipped to the page and saw the list of ways Santa could be killed. Poisoning. Strangulation. Stabbing. Shooting. Dismemberment. Drowning. Electrocution. Fake suicide. Car accident. Pushed off roof. Bludgeoning. Suffocation. Slow torture. Killer bees. Rabid raccoon. Throat cutting. Heart attack. Death by tiger.

Then there were the disclosure details. Did she want her husband to know why he was being killed? If so, did she want it recorded in any way? Did she want to be there? Also, what did she want done with the body? There were myriad choices for her to choose from but it didn't take her long to decide.

"I want you to tell him that I hired you. Then I want him beaten up a little bit and then killed somewhat painlessly. I want the woman dead, too. Just dump their bodies somewhere. In the ocean or something."

Aleph said, "The woman, too? Are you sure? We couldn't find any details on her so I can't say for sure if she even knows he's married."

"I don't care. I'm sick of these stupid sluts fucking anything that moves. They don't care if the guy's married or anything. You'll be doing the world a favor."

"Then consider it done," Aleph said. He was a little apprehensive about killing the woman, not because he had any sort of moral objection to it but because there was something strange about her, something dangerous, and it could all come back to bite him in the ass.

XI.

Aleph watched the woman leave the house.

Through his team of surveillance experts, he found out the woman's name was Kay but that was just about all they found out. There was something about the house that made their surveillance tactics fail on almost every occasion. To make matters worse, nowhere could they find a date of birth, employment history, or anything that any normal human has in terms of a history.

Aleph was bothered by something else. If Santa was having an affair with the woman, why didn't he go with her when she left the house?

Maybe he wasn't having an affair with her. Maybe....

She's holding Santa Claus against his will. But that was impossible. Wasn't it?

It would make sense why his scouts hadn't seen the man ever since he had met the woman. Could he just be hiding out in the house enjoying post-coital bliss? Maybe. But Aleph's instincts told him there was something else. It was important that he find out what that was because if Santa was not being unfaithful, that would change the business arrangement with Mrs. Claus.

Aleph spoke telepathically to his partner Dali who was stationed behind the house. *"New plan. Find a way into the house, identify our target, and verify if the infidelity was consensual."*

Dali answered. *"Will do. You suspect something?"*

"Maybe. Something doesn't seem right. I'm not sure our target wants to be in that house."

"And if that's the case?"

"If that's the case, you let me know and I'll make an executive decision to cancel the hit on our target. I imagine our client will want the woman neutralized but I'll have to verify that."

"Okay. I'm proceeding into the house right now."

"Be careful, Dali."

"Always am."

XII.

Dali entered the backdoor of Kay's house and tripped over a shoebox. Like a cat, he soundlessly caught himself before he fell.

He slowly tip-toed across the floor and perused the room in order to gain more information about the woman who may or may not have kidnapped Santa Claus.

It looked like the typical living room of a single woman except for one thing. In the middle of the floor between the couch and the television, there was a giant snail shell covered in thick, red spirals.

Dali shuddered when he looked at the snail shell. There was something *wrong* about it and it wasn't because it was so out of place. The snail shell started to pulsate and hum.

What the fuck?

Dali quickly slid across the floor away from the shell. He wanted to find Santa Claus and be done with the whole assignment. The humming got louder even though

Dali was getting farther away from the shell. When he made it to the last room down the hallway, the hum was nearly deafening.

Though it was probably not the stealthiest of moves, he barged into the room. He could sense there was someone else in there with him but he didn't see anyone because of the darkness.

Then a muffled voice said, "Let me outta here!"

XIII.

Smitty had never seen Diana so angry.

Sure, he knew that Santa's past indiscretions had affected her but he had been hoping that she'd get over it. He'd also been hoping that the whole thing with the Elves of Fuck was just a coping mechanism, a ritual to help her through the pain and paranoia before she called the whole thing off.

But that wasn't the case.

She was really going to have her husband killed. He almost felt like he should do something about it.

It wasn't that Smitty cared that much about Santa Claus. The truth was the guy was a real asshole, especially to Smitty. It was no secret that Santa didn't like animals. He hated having to rely on the reindeer and had, on more than one occasion, been accused of abusing them. So when Smitty arrived in the North Pole, the big man didn't take too kindly to a hairy humanoid squid making friends with Mrs. Claus.

So now Smitty had to deal with his conflicting emotions. On one hand, he didn't want Diana to have to deal with such a bastard of a husband. On the other hand, the death of Santa Claus would bring about a whole shit storm of trouble for the entire North Pole.

What bothered Smitty the most was the kids. Though he himself never celebrated Christmas, he loved hearing how the holiday brought such happiness to the children of the world. He wasn't even jealous about it. He sincerely enjoyed seeing others happy, especially innocent children.

Smitty saw Diana in front of the toyshop. She was smoking again, which was a bad sign. He slowly approached her and said, "Hey."

Diana quickly flicked the cigarette into a pile of snow. "Oh, hey Smitty."

"Back to smoking, I see."

She frowned. "Sorry."

"You're a big girl. You can do what you want but you know those things are no good for you."

"Neither is a shitty husband."

Smitty looked her straight in the eyes.

"But you're taking care of that, aren't you?"

"Oh my god, Smitty, you're really going to give me a guilt trip now? You know the shit I've been through and you're going to make me feel guilty about finally taking a stand?"

Smitty turned his back to her and was silent for a few seconds. "I'm sorry. I didn't mean to be so nasty. I guess it's just that I disagree with what you decided to do."

"You don't have to agree, Smitty. It's not your marriage. Not your life. You can leave here and it won't make a difference to you. But me? I have to stay."

"Do you want me to leave, Diana?" Smitty said. His tentacles spread out into the snow like a bridal gown.

"Don't be ridiculous. You know that's not what I

meant," Diana said. "I'm tied down to this place. You're free to go wherever you please. I'm not saying I want you to go. I'm just saying that's how it is."

Smitty moved a hairy tentacle up to Diana's face. "I know. I'm sorry. I just wish there was some other way to straighten this whole thing out."

"Me too. You don't think I've thought about it? I have. I've spent months trying to figure out another solution but that bastard just makes it difficult for me. What's done is done. There's no going back."

"That's what I'm afraid of," Smitty said. "That's what I'm afraid of."

XIV.

Dali found the light switch and flicked it on so he could see where the voice was coming from.

In the corner of the room there was a man on the ground, his head enclosed in what looked like a wooden toilet.

"Whoa, what the hell?" Dali said. "Santa, is that you?" He knew it was a stupid question. The man was dressed in the traditional red and white Santa suit. Who the hell else could it be?

"Yes, yes! Who are you? Let me out! I can't move my body!"

Even though his original assignment was to kill Santa, he sort of felt bad for him. The guy was trapped in what looked like a homemade toilet and was paralyzed from the neck down. But that would mean he wasn't in the house by his own free will. The woman had kidnapped him just like Aleph had suspected. That changed everything.

He walked over to the man, pulled away the black silk

that acted as a sort of toilet seat, and peered in.

The man who looked up at him was a far cry from the Santa Claus that Dali imagined. His white beard was covered in red and green globs. His nose was clogged with goo.

"Hold on. I'll get you out." But before Dali could do that, something came into the room and ate him.

XV.

When Santa saw the ugly elf look down at him, he couldn't help but feel embarrassed. He must have looked like hell. But then that didn't matter. He was saved. That is, until he heard something enter the room.

The ugly elf went out of view and what Santa heard made him want to vomit. It sounded like a hundred crabs fighting over a pile of jelly. Then there were the ugly elf's screams muffled every few seconds until they ceased altogether. That was when Santa knew that any chance of his being rescued disappeared along with that ugly elf.

Once the noise died down, the lights went off and whatever had come into the room left.

Santa Claus was left alone in the dark. The globs on his face started to slide off into his ears. Then he heard the voice.

"Open your mouth, Santa. Open and say aaaaaaaaaa-aaaaah!"

XVI.

Though Aleph had cut direct telepathic connection to Dali, he felt the exact moment of his death.

I knew it. I knew something was wrong.

But what? The woman had left the house so did that mean Santa killed Dali? That was difficult to believe. Dali was an expert in both hand-to-hand combat and with throwing knives. That fat bastard Santa would have been no match for the elf.

Aleph tried to initiate contact with Dali, hoping there was still a chance that he was alive, but there was no response.

Dali was dead.

Though his first instinct was to barge into the house and deal with things himself, Aleph knew the wise decision was to call for backup. The situation had to be rectified and the Elves of Fuck always took care of business.

Just as he was going to set up a link to another elf, he saw Kay walk up to the front of the house. Shit was going to hit the fan when she found the dead elf inside.

Better talk with Mrs. Claus first. It's always best to check with the client whenever there's a problem.

Aleph closed his eyes and concentrated on his third eye. With a flash of light he was gone from the hill outside Kay's house and was transported instantly to the North Pole.

He walked down the street, watching the hateful eyes of the Christmas elves. When he reached Diana's house, he saw the squidfoot outside.

Aleph said, "I'm looking for Mrs. Claus."

"So?" Smitty said.

"Can you get her for me?"

"I could."

Aleph stood and waited for the big, hairy thing to go inside to retrieve Diana but instead, it just stood there staring at him. Finally, Aleph said, "Well?"

Smitty took a step forward, his tentacles brushing snow up into a cloud that nearly covered Aleph. "If I was so inclined, yes, I could go get Diana. But I don't take orders from elves." He flicked a tentacle straight up into the air. "Especially *killer* elves."

Aleph took a step forward. He had no time for this shit. "Listen, I don't really know who you are or what kind of relationship you have with Mrs. Claus but my need to speak with her is for her benefit and not mine. So if you care about her even a little bit, you'll go get her or else I'll walk right past you and get her myself. Stand in my way and I'll go *through* you."

There were a few seconds of tense silence and then Smitty said, "Fine. I'll get her."

Aleph watched the squidfoot go into the house. He was relieved it hadn't developed into a physical confrontation. Though he wouldn't have hesitated to kill, Aleph preferred not to do it for free.

Diana walked out and stood on the front porch with her arms crossed. "With all due respect, I don't appreciate your threatening my—"

"Your husband has been abducted, Mrs. Claus," Aleph said. He watched the woman's face turn from annoyed to devastated.

Through tears she said, "By that woman?"

"Yes, that seems to be the case."

Diana said, "So he wasn't cheating on me?"

"Well, I can't say for sure if it started out like that. Maybe he meant to do it and it turned out she was a psycho. I don't know. The point is that he's most likely in real danger now and I'm asking if you want to officially call off the hit. If so, my elves and I will rescue him." Aleph took a step closer. "I have to warn you. There's a chance that your husband may get hurt, or worse."

"What do you mean?"

"If we go in there, it's going to be with guns blazing. I sent in an elf to investigate the situation before we knew for sure. The woman wasn't even in the house. My elf was killed."

"By who? My husband?"

"I doubt it. But this isn't just a regular kidnapping, so I'm warning you. The woman is dangerous. So, officially, do you want to cancel our agreement?"

Diana nodded. "Yes. Please get him back, Aleph. Please."

"I'll do my best." With that, the elf closed his eyes and disappeared. He reappeared on the hill next to Kay's house. He wished he could blow the whole thing up. It had been a long time since he'd worked with explosives.

Aleph had already told Gimel to report to the house. But he wasn't enough. Aleph needed someone who was more dangerous, deadly, and qualified to deal with unusual situations.

He needed the Elf Piercer.

XVII.

Santa watched the dancing sugarplums fart and burp strands of yellow ectoplasm.

He couldn't remember how long he had been locked in the bitch-box but it felt like months. The sugarplums splattered him with more goo, filling his nostrils, his ears, and the corners of his eyes. His mouth was already stuffed with her musty pantyhose that smelled like vinegar.

The ceiling above him was covered in those goddamn sugarplums.

I'd give anything for someone to poke out my eyes. I can't stand looking at those bastards anymore.

A small sugarplum hung from the ceiling on a bright blue spider web. It burped and oozed on Santa's beard. His chin started to tingle and then he heard the clip-clop.

Clip-clop.

Clip-clop.

Kay was coming.

CLIP-clop.

CLIP-CLOP.

"Santa oh Santa!" Kay said, her voice coming from the doorway. She walked slowly up to the box, the clip-clopping getting soft and more sinister. "I have a surprise for you."

Her face appeared above him, blocking out the sugarplums. Santa was again in awe of her beauty despite it being torture just to look at her. She pulled the pantyhose out of his mouth and drooled down his throat.

Santa had no choice but to swallow but there were still remnants in his mouth. He said, "Out."

"What's that? I can barely hear you with all that… mess in your mouth. You say you want out, honey bunch? That's so cute." She leaned forward, drooled onto his lips, and then stuck her fingers into his mouth. "Here, let me wash your mouth out."

Santa sat petrified. More spit. More fingers digging around in his mouth, scrubbing his tongue and teeth with Kay's drool.

"Clean, clean, clean. Squeaky, squeaky clean," she said, making Santa gag with her spit-fingers. "Okay, I think that's enough."

Kay pulled her hand out of his mouth and let Santa gasp for air.

"I'll be right back, honey bunch."

Santa watched her head move away, giving him full view of the sugarplums. They seemed to have multiplied. Dozens of them were circling him, farting their ectoplasm into the air. Star and circle shapes formed out of the goo until they coalesced into a giant wheel that started to turn.

A wheel? Can I make a unicycle out of it? A unicycle made out of sugarplum shit. That's a good one. It'll be next year's hottest toy.

A smaller wheel appeared in the middle of the big one. Each one turned in the opposite direction, creating a wind that blew the sugarplums across the room and away from Santa much to his delight.

Thank you, sugarplum-shit unicycle. Thank you.

XVIII.

Shaw, also known as the Elf Piercer, packed his weapons: two long chains with meat hooks on the ends of them. It had been a long time since they'd tasted some meat. It was going to be a good day.

It had also been a while since Shaw was called for an assignment. He had usually been reserved for only the most dangerous missions because he had the tendency to go overboard. From what he was told about the target, Shaw knew that going overboard might just be what was necessary.

Shaw looked at himself in the mirror. "Hell yeah," he said. He closed his eyes and teleported to the location Aleph had specified.

He arrived instantly to find Aleph and Gimel waiting for him.

Shaw nodded at the two of them.

Aleph said, "It's been a while since I've required the skills of the Elf Piercer."

"No one really calls me that anymore," Shaw said. "It's a pretty stupid nickname."

Gimel gestured toward Shaw's weapons. "I think it's well-deserved."

"No one asked you," Shaw said.

"I'm just saying. You're the only elf to ever—"

"Shut the hell up, Gimel!" Aleph said. "We're here to take care of business, not discuss ancient history."

Gimel shrugged. "Whatever. Let's do this."

Aleph looked at Shaw. "You ready?"

"Yeah."

Gimel cocked his guns. He put on the glove he reserved for special jobs: a glove made out of bone and shaped like a monstrous penis. Those elves in Tokyo sure knew how to construct a weapon of torture.

Shaw, the Elf Piercer, grabbed a chain with each hand and pulled them off his belt. The hooks were newly sharpened and shined in the moonlight. "I can't wait to get my hooks wet," he said. "Nice and wet."

Aleph looked at the other two and was glad he had them on his side. In recent months, the Elves of Fuck had gone through quite a bit of downsizing due to the economy. The company simply could not afford to have as many elves on the payroll as in the past and the elves that were on the payroll were paid on a job-to-job basis. The concept of salary-elves was gone.

Though not as creatively armed as Gimel or Shaw, Aleph had a weapon that had proved its worth over the years: the actual sword used by Saturnalia at the Battle of

Xaman. The sword, crafted out of black elephant bone, was taller than Aleph but he could wield the weapon like a master swordsman.

"Gimel, you take the back. Shaw, you have the side that's facing us. I'll come through the front," Aleph said.

"Are we teleporting in or what?" Gimel said.

"Yeah. We need the element of surprise. Dali couldn't teleport and maybe that's why they were able to get him. I'll be honest with you. There's something weird about that house so I can't promise you what's going to happen in there. So let's get ready. On the count of three we go." He closed his eyes.

"One."

Shaw closed his eyes.

"Two."

Gimel closed his eyes.

"Three."

All three elves disappeared in flashes of light.

XIX.

Tortured by an angel. If I ever get out of here and have a chance to make a TV show, that's what it's going to be called.

Santa was mentally numb to the sugarplums and to the drool clogging nearly every facial orifice. He just wanted out of there.

Santa heard Kay's footsteps. There was the usual clip-clopping and then something different. A slapping sound on the hardwood floor.

Her face appeared above him. "Guess what? I have a surprise for you."

"Errrrrrrrrrrrrr," was all Santa could say.

"You see, honey bunch, if you have been paying attention you know I've been wearing my high heels this whole time. They look great on me, don't you agree?" She slapped him in the face. "Right?"

"Errrrrrrrrrrr!"

Kay bent down, picked up her shoes and held them up so Santa could see. "These here glittery beauties have been on my feet for *six days*. And when I say six days I mean twenty-four hours a day. You see, Santa my dear, I don't sleep. Never had to, never wanted to. So I have worn these shoes all day for six days." She brought a shoe to her nose and smelled the inside. "Ewww, what a god-awful smell! Really, really rank. Does that turn you on? A woman with smelly feet?"

"Errrrrrrrrrrr!"

"Well, it doesn't matter because I'm giving them to you. Such sweet, sweet gifts…from me…." She brought one of the shoes closer to Santa. "To you."

Santa had recalled Kay's shoes being gorgeous and glittery like Dorothy's shoes in The Wizard of Oz. But now, with a clear view of the insides of the shoes, they were anything but gorgeous and glittery. Instead, they looked dark and moist, stained with days and days of foot sweat. Then he wondered if perhaps Dorothy's shoes looked the same after all those hours of filming the movie.

Why am I thinking about The Wizard of Oz? Dorothy wasn't a sadistic angel. She never locked anyone in a bitch-box. Or maybe she did. I don't know.

Kay moved the shoes to his face in slow motion, prolonging the torture and letting the stench waft to his nostrils. Despite being clogged with drool, Santa's nose didn't block the smell.

"Yum, I bet you can really smell that shit, right?" Kay said. "You should be honored, too. Oh, not only because they are my shoes in your face, even though that *should* be enough. No sir, you should also be honored that you have an authentic pair of vintage *Babs Cloantas* in your face. You just cannot find shoes like these anymore."

Santa said, "Errrrrrrrr." He thought about his wife and how she never once talked about what kind of shoes she wore. Diana wasn't into that sort of thing, never put value on something as insignificant as shoes.

The reek of Kay's foot sweat bore through Santa's nose, up to his brain, and down to his throat. The odor made its home in his mouth so that now the taste of her drool mingled with the warm stink from her shoes.

"Hope you're enjoying this shit, honey bunch. There's a lot more where this came from. I have nearly five-thousand pairs of shoes and you'll get to smell each and every one. Not just heels, though. I have clogs and sneakers and slippers and mules and flip-flops…"

Kay's voice became heavy syrup on Santa's ears. It became sticky syrup that seeped into his ear canals and covered his brain, erasing all memory of his wife and his position as Santa Claus, deliverer of gifts. Combined with her foot stink, her voice made him a masochistic automaton.

"You're mine now, honey bunch," Kay said, dropping the shoes and leaving them next to Santa's head. "All mine."

XX.

When Gimel teleported inside, the first thing he noticed was the ugly giant snail shell in the middle of the living room. Who does that? It was such a foolish decision in interior decorating.

He had his gun in one hand and his glove on the other, ready for anything. The house was silent but Gimel could hear the quiet thoughts of Aleph and Shaw. They were thinking the same thing he was: the objects in the house were strange as hell.

As he tip-toed out of the living room and into the hallway, his ears popped. Something in his skull clicked and he no longer heard the thoughts of his fellow elves.

Aleph, can you hear me? Shaw?

No response.

A slimy chill on the back of his neck tickled him. Gimel turned quickly but a wet slap sent him flying to the ground. He looked up and saw the same snail shell but now it was standing on what looked like two chicken legs. It wasn't a snail, though. It looked more like the result of a snail mating with an elephant. Several trunk-like appendages waved at him, gaping holes hungry for fresh elf meat. Gimel held his gun up and fired.

The bullet hit the snail-thing right in the middle of its body but had no effect. Gimel sent another one at its head but again: nothing. The snail-thing stepped closer, its trunks sending out sound waves that popped Gimel's ears even more.

Gimel stood up. "You ugly piece of shit," he said, getting his glove arm ready to do some damage. The weapon was usually reserved for punishing unfaithful spouses of his clients. The sheer size of the bone-penis glove struck fear into the hearts of both males and females. When that thing went in, even the most jaded of infidels felt the pangs of conscience.

The snail-thing waved its trunks, spraying Gimel with purple spittle. Some of the fluid hit the elf in the face, burning him. He put his fist up and charged.

The bone-penis smashed into the snail shell, creating a splatter of green and white shards.

Gimel's fist went right through the beast. Trunks flailed against the elf, wrapping around his neck.

"No you don't, fucker," Gimel said. He pulled his fist out and started punching at the trunks. They were no match for it.

Two more minutes of fisting and the elf was victorious in turning the snail-thing into a mushy pile of shell and flesh. Gimel's deafness gradually disappeared as the beast before him died.

XXI.

While Gimel was walking through the living room, Shaw was in another room trying to comprehend why someone would decorate their walls with pictures of rotting fruit, demolished buildings, umbrellas, and airplanes. In the corner, there was a bed made of red metallic goop that resembled dried up taffy.

What kind of weird bitch lives here?

He had a chain in each hand, swinging them slowly so the hooks would be ready to carve into flesh at a moment's notice.

There were slobbering sounds coming from the next room so Shaw walked slowly, one hook swinging behind his head. As he walked through the doorway, something fell from above and covered his head like a Halloween mask. He couldn't see and could barely breathe.

"Shit!" he said, dropping one of the chains and grabbing at whatever was wrapped around his head. His fingers dug into soft, gritty flesh. It wasn't working. Shaw started biting at it, grinding the flesh between his teeth until he felt air on his tongue.

He dropped the other chain and used two hands to rip the thing off him. Before another could drop on him, he grabbed both chains and looked at what he'd thrown off. It was a giant sugarplum.

On the floor, the fruit was torn apart but still trembling with life. It resembled road kill and Shaw almost felt bad for it. Then he looked up. The entire ceiling was covered in giant, bulbous sugarplums.

Some were hairy. Some had tiny legs. Some were on fire. Each of them seemed to be staring at Shaw even though they possessed no eyes.

"You gotta be kidding me," Shaw said. He swung one of his chain hooks over his head and let it go in the direction of the sugarplums. They scattered like roaches as the hooks cut into several of them.

The sugarplums that were hit fell to the ground, wounds gaping multicolored blood and fruit viscera. The scurrying survivors flew into the air and surrounded Shaw as he swung his second chain hook over his head. A sugarplum with an appendage that resembled an axe flew directly at him, but Shaw managed to duck just in time. He swung his weapon and managed to hit a dozen more, sending chunks everywhere.

One of those chunks landed right in Shaw's mouth and slid down his throat.

"Goddamnit!" he said, nearly choking. It only took a few seconds for it to take effect.

As he stared at the room full of sugarplums, the colors grew brighter until everything was overly saturated. The walls turned to liquid, the sugarplums turned to fiery monster faces, and furniture made of chicken legs appeared in the middle of the room. A table shook, the grains in the wood cracking to form a mouth. It said, "Come have a seat, have a seat, have a seat…"

Shaw closed his eyes. Using only his instinct, he swung both chain hooks while spinning in a circle, hoping to kill each and every sugarplum or talking piece of furniture in the room.

He felt his hooks hit things but couldn't tell what they hit. Finally, he dropped to the floor in exhaustion. "Just fucking kill me," he said. He felt a sugarplum crawl onto his face and fart, sending poison gas down his throat.

The Elf Piercer was dead.

XXII.

While his partners were fighting their own battles, Aleph walked through the front part of the house. He tried to keep telepathic communication open but could only hear muffled voices.

The room he was in looked like it was decorated by a madman or in this case, a madwoman. Wigs of every color and style were hung on the walls and dozens of model airplanes dangled from the ceiling. The furniture consisted of large metal barrels covered in lacy throw pillows.

Aleph held his sword poised for action.

This assignment had really turned sour. When he was first asked to join the Elves of Fuck, he was eager for the adventure. Correcting infidelities through surveillance and violence seemed like a fun way to earn money. Aleph had always taken his job seriously, but he was starting to lose the passion and heart he'd had in his early years with the company. To make matters worse, because of recent budget cuts, he felt it was harder to justify the hard work with the meager salary.

This will be the last job and then I find something else. I take care of this crazy bitch, rescue Santa Claus, and then I'm out.

As Aleph walked into the next room, he saw Santa Claus standing against the wall, smiling.

"Santa?" the elf said. "Are you okay? Your wife hired me. I'm here to rescue you."

"Errrrrrrrrrrrrrrr!" Santa said. He took a few steps forward and that's when Aleph smelled the peppermint.

The woman must have been standing there the entire time but Aleph hadn't seen her. For the first time in years, Aleph felt himself aroused by the sight of a human woman. She was beautiful. Simply beautiful.

He was eye-level with her massive breasts. They called to him. *Bury yourself in us…Lick the sweat from underneath these mountains.*

Aleph shook himself loose from the woman's mental grasp and ran forward with his sword. The woman dodged out of the way like a sexy cheetah.

"Oh, look. It's a naked little elf," she said, sending a fist to the back of Aleph's head. Again he slashed with his blade and managed to cut Kay across the arm. Her blood fell to the floor with a splat.

The blood bubbled and grew into several chunks of hairy, black flesh. They rolled in front of Santa Claus, who was still grinning like an idiot.

Kay said, "Oh, look at what you've done, you dumb little thing." She punched at the elf again but Aleph blocked the attack with his arm.

The woman was strong. Aleph's head hurt like hell but he still slashed several times at Kay, missing each time. She was fast, too.

Finally, he said, "What the fuck did you do to him?"

Kay laughed. "Whatever do you mean? What makes you think I did anything to him? He and I are lovers, you know. Have been for years. Who are you to get in the way of true love?" She walked over to the chunks of flesh and spat on them.

Aleph was about to rush her again when he saw the chunks start to grow until they were the size of infants. The pieces of hairy flesh formed into miniature apes with red faces.

Kay proudly stood next to them. "Here you go, little elf. Meet the red faces of god!"

The apes ran to Aleph, grunting and pounding their little fists in the air. He slashed down with his sword, catching one of the creatures in the head. Its split skull opened up and spat out sugarplums. Another slash of the sword and two apes were decapitated. Their tiny heads rolled to Kay's feet. She screamed.

"How dare you!"

Seeing her rage only made Aleph more determined to hack his way through the angry apes. One of them got to Aleph and grabbed his penis. It pulled and pulled while the elf pounded the ape's head with the handle of his sword. "For fuck's sake, get the hell off my dick!"

The red-faced ape grinned and pulled harder. Finally, there was the tearing of flesh and Aleph's penis was ripped off and in the ape's mouth.

Kay laughed. She jumped forward and grabbed Aleph's neck. Face to face with the woman, the elf could smell her sweet peppermint breath.

"Oh, you'd fit perfectly in my bitch-box. You want to be my bitch, dear?" she said. "Drink my piss, eat my—"

Kay screamed.

Aleph hadn't seen Gimel walk into the room. He hadn't seen the elf take his giant bone-penis glove and shove it up Kay's skirt. But that's what happened.

Kay's hands dropped from Aleph's neck and she fell to her knees with Gimel's hand still inside her. "Get the fuck out of me!" she screamed.

Gimel was in a trance. He pushed his fist in, pulled it out a tiny bit, and shoved it in again, deeper and harder than before. Kay let out a howl like a dying baboon.

Once he got his bearings, Aleph brought his sword up and brought it down on the woman's neck.

Kay's head rolled over to Santa's feet. Her neck gushed sugarplums that smelled like peppermint and menstrual blood.

"Fucking hell," Gimel said.

"Yeah." Aleph dropped his sword and fell over, exhausted. He looked over at Santa. The jolly, fat man was still staring into space, grinning like an idiot.

XXIII.

"He's a goddamn zombie!" Diana shouted. "Look at him! He just sits there all day, drooling and mumbling about that woman!"

Smitty listened to Diana as she vented. It had been a week since Christmas and Santa showed no sign of getting better. "I know, Diana. I'm sorry."

"All day I have to hear about her beautiful tits, her delicious spit, her heavenly piss. I swear if I have to hear about it one more time, I'm going to kill myself."

"Take it easy, Diana. Aleph's going to be here any minute. He said he'd see if there was a way to help Santa so let's just wait and see. No use getting more upset until we know if there's anything we can do."

Diana sighed. "Yeah, I know."

There was a flash of light and Aleph stood in front of them, naked and with a bandage over his crotch. "Hello Mrs. Claus...Mr. Smitty."

"What'd you find out?" Diana said.

"Well," Aleph said. "Kay, the woman who kidnapped your husband, we couldn't find anything more on her even after we did the initial search of the house. But here's the weird part. A few days later we went back to the town, only to find that the town had...disappeared."

Diana's jaw fell open. "What are you talking about?"

"The town...I knew there was something strange about it, but I didn't think it was that significant. I thought it was limited only to Kay. But now it's as if the town was never there."

Smitty said, "Maybe you guys weren't checking the right place. Maybe you got lost or something."

"No," Aleph said. "The city of Tusk never existed, at least not in that form. We did find some other information...about a small village named Tusk from the fourth century. It may or may not be related to our situation."

"What? What about it?" Diana said.

"Nevermind that. It's not going to help your situation." Aleph didn't want to go into detail and risk having a vengeful wife on his hands. "I do have good news, though."

Diana's face got considerably less upset. "What? Is my husband going to get better?"

"Well, yeah. But it's a good news, bad news sort of thing."

Smitty spoke up. "What's the good news?"

"The good news is Mr. Claus will go back to his old self."

Diana looked hesitant. "And the bad news?"

Aleph sighed. "It's going to take about five years."

XXIV.

Diana handed Smitty a bottle of beer. "So, did you think about it?"

"Yeah. All night."

"So?"

"I don't know. I haven't made a decision," he said. "What do you think?"

"It's not the type of decision I can make for you."

"I know." Smitty drank the beer in one gulp. "But a squidfoot delivering Christmas presents? That's the most ridiculous thing I've ever heard."

"But it's only for five years."

"Ha! Only for five years," Smitty said. He threw the beer bottle into the trash and started to pace back and forth.

"You like kids, don't you? You always say you like seeing them happy?"

"Yeah...."

"Well then?"

Smitty sighed, his tentacles drooping to the floor. "But what if I'm no good at it? What if I ruin Christmas for everyone?"

Diana stood up and put her arms around him. She gestured to a large box in the middle of the room. "Then I'll put you in my bitch-box."

Smitty laughed and kissed her back. He put his face into her hair and inhaled her scent. His nose wiggled.

Diana had always smelled so nice, but there was something different this time. Was it a new shampoo? A new perfume? What was that smell?

Was that...*peppermint?*

FROSTY

and

the Full Monty

BY

Jeff Burk

Jeff Burk *is a guy I drink with regularly. He's a diehard punk with a dreaded mohawk who's always excited to talk about gore movies, Star Trek, Grant Morrison comics, and crack rock steady bands. He is the author of the bestselling bizarro book,* Shatnerquake, *about William Shatner battling other William Shatners Die Hard style. He's also written the choose your own adventure parody* Super Giant Monster Time *and the forthcoming books* HomoBomb *and* Pot Head. *When I mentioned I wanted to do this Christmas anthology, he claimed the Frosty story. He said, "I don't know what I'm going to write yet, but I want to put Frosty through hell." I told him to go for it. Frosty had it coming to him.*

So sit back with a nice glass of brandy eggnog and enjoy this tale of the snowman who was brought to life with a little Christmas magic . . .

Frosty the Snowman stepped onto the stage for the third time that night. With one icy hand he grabbed the stripper pole and swung his hips to Bing Crosby's voice crooning over the club's PA system.

A gang of bikers crowded the club. Every seat was filled with tattooed, leather jacketed, pierced members of The Crack Pipe Kings Motorcycle Club. They had been here all night, just like last night and the night before.

Frosty didn't know why they were always there. He figured they liked the girls of the club and he was a snow-*man*. But he seemed to be their favorite and they did tip very well.

The stage lights illuminated his snow body and the crowd went wild. They cheered, clanked beers, and head butted each other in excitement.

Frosty the snowman was a jolly happy soul.

Blue sequin bikini briefs glittered in the spotlight on his pelvis. The light was hot and Frosty could feel his snow beginning to melt. Fortunately, his dances were only four minutes long.

He began to dance around.

That was his cue. He turned slowly, facing the audience, reached down sliding his finger under the special Velcro strap and quickly tore off the briefs revealing his smooth snowman physique. Frosty ground his hips against the pole and the audience roared.

***

Karen, Jackie, Billy and June were building a magnificent snowman. He was almost as tall as the stop sign he was next to. They had given him two pieces of coal for eyes, a red button for a nose, and even a corncob pipe.

The last touch was the black silk hat that Karen had found. It was hard to reach, but with help from Jackie and Billy, Karen got the hat on top of the snowman's head.

All four children stepped back to admire their creation, straight into the path of an oncoming snowplow. The driver wasn't paying that close of attention, he was shitfaced. All four bodies were very small so there wasn't even a thump as they got over taken by snow and pushed by the plow. They were crushed into a large mound of ice and their bodies weren't discovered for two weeks.

It turned out there was a little magic in that old silk hat they found. The snowman they had built leapt to life and began to dance around.

A bum walking by yelled "Yay! It's Frosty!"

Frosty waved back. "Good Day, Sir."

He went walking down the street, as happy as could be. Everyone waved at him and shouted greetings as he strolled by.

He came to an alleyway and there was a very skinny man wearing a very dirty trench coat leaning against the wall.

"Good day, Sir," said Frosty.

The man, whose name was Alan, beamed the biggest smile he had in years. Instantly, he was transported back to those childhood Christmases and remembered how in-between his dad beating him and putting out cigarettes on his arms, he would escape into the magic of those television specials: *Rudolph the Red Nose Reindeer*, *A Garfield Christmas* and his favorite, *Frosty the Snowman*.

So Alan offered Frosty the one thing he had.

"Hey Frosty, wanna do some ice?"

Frosty assumed, since he was a snowman, that "ice" must be something good for him. He did not know what was being offered was methamphetamine.

Frosty hit the pipe and the drug went straight to his head and heart. Euphoria overtook him, he loved it! As it turns out, snowmen are quite addiction-prone. Frosty was instantly addicted.

* * *

Bing Crosby stopped singing and the PA began to blast The Beach Boys' rendition of "Frosty the Snowman." The sweet sixties pop had been specially remixed by the Club's DJ to include a booty-shaking, boot-stomping bass line.

The bikers cheered louder, this was their favorite song for Frosty to dance to and every set he did ended this way.

A skinny and sickly looking biker climbed onto the stage and rushed at Frosty. His lust making him forget proper club decorum.

From the shadows, two obese bouncers moved with surprising agility grabbing the biker. They lifted him up, one putting him in a headlock and the other grabbing his legs. They carried him off the stage and through a door. The stage invader would be found in the hospital the next morning. This was not the first time the club had to aggressively enforce the no-touching rule. It was that kind of club.

The rest of the gang paid no mind, their beer-and-boner-goggles keeping them enraptured with Frosty and his stage show.

* * *

So Frosty spent his days smoking and hanging in alleys with other bums and wastes of life, and it was a happy time. Each day blended into the next in his drug haze and Alan and Frosty became the best of friends.

But one day the money ran out and Frosty and Alan found themselves with handguns holding up a liquor store. The store clerk had a shotgun. The first shot took Alan's head clean off, splattering the snowman with blood and brains. But when the clerk turned the gun on Frosty, the buckshot passed through Frosty's torso of snow with no ill effect.

Frosty fired back and ran, leaving the clerk to bleed out. In a short time he was caught. The red-stained snow made it an open and shut case.

On his first day in federal prison, he was cornered by a group of Crips. They mistook the blood stains in his snow for Frosty reppin' the wrong colors. They formed a circle around him and pushed him back and forth hurling insults. In the jostle his hat got knocked off and Frosty immediately turned back into a plain old snowman.

When a guard finally put his hat back on, Frosty found himself covered in sticky, white goo. After a trip to the med ward and a few meetings with the prison counselor, Frosty understood what happened to him.

That was how he learned to perform "snowjobs."

He used this peculiar talent to get through his time

in prison. He was able to trade snowjobs for protection, smokes, and when the prison served ice cream, extra dessert. This gift to leave his body proved vital for the survival a snowman who, for some unknown reason, aroused the lust of the biggest and meanest inmates.

* * *

Frosty sat in his private freezer/dressing room. The club owner had been nice enough to build a special room for Frosty to refreeze his snow after every dance.

Frosty took a drag from a cigarette and placed it into the ashtray on his dresser. He looked at his reflection in the mirror. The years had been hard on him; his once pure white snow was now an ugly grey.

In front of the mirror was his only personal possession, the corncob pipe he came to life with. He thought of all he had been through and all he had smoked with that pipe: meth, crack, marijuana, and on the rare occasion, tobacco.

There was a knock at the door and Cinnamon poked her head in.

"You got a private customer in booth three," she said and shut the door.

Frosty sighed and took a hit of ice from his corncob pipe.

He stood up and left the room. The private booths were just down the hall, each one labeled one through six. Frosty walked into number three.

* * *

Eventually his sentence was up and Frosty's debt to society was paid. But what was a living snowman with no job skills and a criminal record to do?

He found that his snowjob skill from prison had use on the outside as well. In no time at all, Frosty was trading snowjobs for his precious ice.

One day he was lying in an alley, the same alley where so many years ago he met Alan, stoned out of his head when a fat greasy man walked by. The man stopped when he saw the snowman. This man owned *Jezebel's,* the city's most notorious strip club.

He had been looking for something new for the club, something to revive customer interest and looking at the down on his luck snowman, he had an idea.

The man helped Frosty to his feet.

"Hey kid, I gotta business proposition for you."

* * *

The booth was small, barely enough room for the burly biker and the portly snowman. The walls were lined with mirrors and a single bare light bulb hung from the ceiling.

Over the room's private speakers, Alvin and the Chipmunks were singing.

And the children say he could laugh and play just the same as you and me.

That damn song. It didn't matter what time of year or what month it was. His customers always requested the same song. Sometimes different artists—The Jackson 5, The Ronettes, Ella Fitzgerald, Cocteau Twins, Fiona Apple

—but always the same damn song.

Frosty wondered all the time about the song. Was there another snowman that came to life before him? Was that one lucky to lead a happy life? Or was it really about him? Everyone did call him "Frosty."

The biker stood up and approached Frosty. No matter how hard he tried, Frosty never got used to this. He felt the heat of the lightbulb above his head. A tear ran from his button eye but was indistinguishable from the just beginning to form slush.

The biker kissed Frosty softly on his lips of coal. Flecks of snow dotted his bushy beard. He gently removed Frosty's hat and unbuckled his pants, preparing for his snowjob.

a. Goldfarb presents OCNER STUMP'S ONE THOUSAND SORROWS

No. 30 — "Unwanted Gifts"

Fin.

TWO-WAY SANTA

BY

Kevin L. Donihe

Kevin L. Donihe is one of the originators of the bizarro fiction genre. He was there in the beginning. He's one of the most intelligent human beings I've ever met, as well one of the most eccentric. Whenever you're around him you feel as if you're hanging out with a younger version of Hunter S. Thompson as portrayed by Johnny Depp in Fear and Loathing in Las Vegas. Although his books have yet to be among Eraserhead Press's bestsellers, those who have read his work always rate him as one of the best. From House of Houses, about a man who is so in love with his house that he goes to house heaven to be with her after the great house apocalypse tears them apart, to Washer Mouth, about a washing machine who becomes human in order to meet his favorite soap opera star. There is no writer on the planet quite like him.

In this Christmas on Crack story, Donihe shows us the more tender side of Santa Claus. It's a very special down and out Miracle on 34th Street type of tale that will surely warm your heart through the snowy Christmas eve . . .

It was a few minutes past final call when I first met Santa Claus. I'm a nice guy, you see. I often take homeless men back with me to my apartment and let them sleep there for a day or two, sometimes longer. It's according to how I feel about them, and how they make me feel.

On the street, there was hardly any traffic. On the sidewalk: no pedestrians other than me. My fellow drinkers, freshly expelled from the taproom, had all gotten into their cars. They weren't comfortable walking alone this late at night, but I felt at home amongst broken buildings, broken people.

Once the roar of engines faded, I turned my attention to the little things: the sound of refuse blowing in alleyways, the pattern of lights in apartment windows and concrete as it exuded steam from a recent rain. Beneath my feet, pavement felt strangely soft and giving. Traffic lights up ahead jiggled or looked like dancing smears.

Turning a corner, I noticed something slumped against an alley wall. It looked like a sack of garbage, ignored by the sanitation crew. I thought I knew what was hiding under all that voluminous, dirty fabric, though. And I was right. I regarded Santa. His overcoat encased him like an unzipped body bag, only woolen. His beard was long, white and flowing. A streetlight made his face seem the color of piss. He was old, too—one of the oldest homeless guys I'd seen wandering these parts. I wondered how long he'd been living in alleys in cardboard boxes, or defecating in weeds behind the old strip mall up the road.

Santa had a tart, almost gamy smell. Closer, I noted an all but empty bottle, clutched in his bony right hand.

"Is that whiskey?" I asked.

The man nodded, but made no attempt at eye contact. He appeared to contemplate the pavement. Maybe not even that.

"Looks like you don't have much left," I said, "but I could get you more."

He looked up then, his eyes deep-set, lost in shadow. "You'd do that for me?"

"Of course. But you'll have to leave this alley."

"Where would I go?"

"To my place," was my reply.

He studied me, seemed to think. "Did you say whiskey? *Free* whiskey?"

"Totally free." I paused a beat. "Will you come?"

"Sure, buddy. I'm game." He stood then, knees shaking. Quickly, he grasped the wall to avoid a swift return to the pavement.

I offered him my hand. "Need help?"

"No, I'll make it."

I marveled. The man had a trace of dignity left in him after all.

* * *

It took ten minutes to traverse the two blocks from the alley in which I'd found my new friend. He was slow, and the way he hobbled behind me made me wonder if one of his legs was gimpy.

I couldn't let him stagger all the way back to my apartment. At his rate, it would take us an hour to reach. I was ready to get back and show this man both my place and my hospitality, so I steadied him, invited him to lean on my shoulder. He didn't resist me. In fact, he seemed grateful for this small act of kindness.

"What's your name?" I asked.

He just mumbled.

* * *

An hour later, I was watching TV; the man was laid out on my bed. He'd fallen asleep almost immediately upon lying down. He snored loudly. I would have checked on him, intermittently, if not for the snoring. The noise let me know he was okay, that he hadn't swallowed his tongue or choked on his own vomit.

The snores stopped at some point. A minute or so later, I heard the creak of bedsprings.

I turned off the TV in the middle of a show. I walked to the bedroom and saw Santa sitting on the bed, legs dangling, his eyes tilted down, looking at the bedspread much like he'd looked at the pavement earlier.

"Feeling better?" I asked.

"I'd feel better if I had another drink," he said, and met my gaze then. In the light, I could better see his eyes—gray and rheumy. One had an obvious cataract. "You promised me a drink, didn't you?"

"I did." I walked to a wooden chest at the foot of the bed and opened it. Fifteen bottles of booze were inside, all for this man and others like him yet to make my acquaintance. I selected one of the whiskey bottles—expensive stuff, seal unbroken—and lifted it so the man might see.

For the first time, I noticed some life in him. His long,

thin arms reached out to me as his hands clutched the air. "Can I have it now?"

I handed him the bottle, smiled. "Of course."

He ripped off the plastic wrapper and cracked the seal. Before drinking, he smelled the whiskey, like a taster. But he didn't merely taste it; he downed a fifth of the bottle before drawing a breath.

I pulled up a chair across from him, took a seat. Crossing my legs, I asked, "So, what's your story?"

"What?"

"Everyone has a story. I want to know yours."

He belched, wiped his lips. "Why do you care?"

That was a good question. I wasn't sure why I cared. Maybe I didn't and just wanted a little conversation to elevate my mood. "Humor me," I said after a few moments. "I gave you that whole bottle, after all." Then I gestured to the walls. "And this place for the night..."

"If that's what you want," he said. "But you might not believe it."

Anticipatory tingles started in my fingertips. "Try me."

"Okay." He paused for another drink, then, "I'm Father Christmas."

"Father Christmas?" I uncrossed my legs, leaned in closer. "Like Santa Claus, you mean?"

"Yeah, like Santa Claus, but I preferred Father Christmas." He paused. "Back *then*, at least. You can call me whatever you want now."

It seemed he was one of the crazy homeless men. Interesting, sure—but I'd hosted a number of them recently, and not enough of the quiet, shy or sweet types. Still, he didn't strike me as the kind of fellow I'd have to toss out prematurely, so I played along: "I thought Santa—excuse me, Father Christmas—lived at the North Pole."

"Yeah, that's right. *Lived.*"

"So, what happened? Mrs. Claus kick you out?"

"No, nothing like that. I'd been growing sick of things for years, and it just came to a head. I mean, doing all that shit for people who'll stop believing in you—it's fucking depressing!"

"What did Mrs. Claus think when you left?"

He threw up his hands, sloshing the whiskey. "Nothing! She'd been senile for the last two hundred years! Spent all of her time alone in a rocking chair in the attic. She'd put the chair over a loose floorboard, just above my bedroom. I wore earplugs, but I always heard it. Always and forever."

"Couldn't you have gotten a divorce?"

His eyes widened. He seemed aghast. "Santa? *Divorced*? Hell no!" Eyes narrowed. "But Mrs. Claus can dry up and turn to dust for all I care."

"So you've never returned, not even for a visit?"

His tone was matter-of-fact. "When I left, I left for good."

I paused, thought for a bit. "If that's the case, why are people still receiving your gifts?"

"It's contracted out. Some firm in Asia is doing it now."

"What happened to the elves?"

"Most were transferred to circuses."

"And the reindeer?"

"They were…dispatched." He gulped some whiskey. "Hope I'm not boring you."

"Oh no! Not at all!" Indeed, I was intrigued by his ramblings, and rather taken by the man himself. He was by far the most articulate homeless person I'd encountered, and I felt a little guilty for having lumped him in with others more prosaically crazy. "So, you quit being Santa to live on the streets. That's what you're saying, right?"

"No," he said. "You're leaving out the middle."

"I am? Fill me in, then."

After yet another drink: "I was sick of the cold, so I moved to LA. Got a job as a waiter, thinking I might get lucky with an acting career. I mean, plenty of actors have played me—but all I got were doors slammed in my face." He sighed, looked wistful. "Eventually, I landed a gig directing a string of porn films under the name Roger Wood. Ever see them?"

"I don't watch porn," I said. "Too indirect."

"Me, neither. It was just a way to make a living."

I leaned forward. "But you're not directing porn now. What happened?"

"Staged sex jaded me; I tried working an office job. But I'm old and not made for the 9-to-5 grind. Couldn't take that little bastard of a boss, either. Mr. McCullough was his name. Fucker.

"I even tried working in fast food, but nothing brought me joy. I had to break away from it all—The North Pole, LA, life in general. 12 years ago, I dropped the Santa-shtick; 6 years ago, I became a bum." He looked down at his hands. "I am what I am. Take it or leave it."

I smiled. "I took it, didn't I?"

"Guess you did…"

As he drank more whiskey, I replayed our little conversation in my head. Though the man told an interesting tale, in no way did I believe it at the time. Still, the experience had been fun, and maybe a touch rewarding. I hadn't heard so colorful a story from a homeless man since one claimed last year to not only be President but also a time-traveling alien. Rising from the chair, I made my way to the bed and sat beside my friend. I gestured to the bottle in his hand. "You don't mind if I have a sip, do you?"

"It's yours, isn't it?"

I took it, downed a gulp and imagined my spit intermingling with Santa's. After handing the bottle back to him, I made a show of stretching my arms and yawning. Then I lay down on the left side of the bed, head on the pillow.

"You can do the same," I told him.

He seemed hesitant. He looked down at the bottle. "I'm not finished yet."

"Save some for later," I said. "I'm not going to hurt you." Then I patted the opposite pillow. "Just lie down. Relax."

He looked from the whiskey to the pillow and back again. Finally, he put the bottle on the nightstand and stretched out awkwardly beside me. His tired old body seemed to resist the reclined position. Knees wouldn't bend fully; his back arced slightly. Neck, too.

I touched his hand, the nape of his neck. He felt so cold. I decided I'd be a Good Samaritan and donate a little of my body warmth to him.

We spooned silently for so long I began to feel drowsy. I looked over at the clock. It wasn't even 3 AM yet.

"I'm tired of lying around," I said, my voice a whisper. "Aren't you?"

"No, it's soft here," he replied, his voice cracking with

phlegm. "I'm not used to soft."

"Okay," I said. "We can keep doing this. Guess I owe you, after that entertaining story you told."

"It wasn't a story."

I sat up a bit. "But I can't believe you. See, I know exactly where my presents came from. Mom and Dad and the aunts and uncles—they bought them in stores, wrapped them up and put little bows on top. Same story every year."

He turned around and faced me. "I never claimed all the presents were mine," he said. "Usually, a kid got one of my gifts every three or four years. But if I gave one, it was always the kid's favorite."

"Three or four years?" I said. "Your *Bad List* must have been huge."

"It wasn't that they'd been bad. It's just that other kids had been better, and I didn't have time to go to every house." He paused, looked so deeply into my eyes I almost flinched. "You were a little better than most. You got four before you turned ten, but you didn't get another until you were 24." He half-smiled. "That was my last delivery."

"Wait. You delivered to adults?"

"It wouldn't be fair if I'd just given them to kids, would it? Adults deserved a little magic too."

He still stared at me. I wanted to turn away, but there was something behind his eyes, something that shimmered, and it tried to convince me that what he was saying was true. Conflicting thoughts began to churn inside my head. For a moment, I felt like blubbering.

I composed myself. "So, if you're really Santa, what was my favorite gift when I was five?" I paused, smirked. "Or was that too long ago for you to remember?"

"One thing I've got is my memory." He tapped his head. "Every present that everyone has ever received from me is locked up here. I can't forget them, even if I tried. That year, you wanted, more than anything, a yellow toy truck." His eyes twinkled, but it was a melancholy twinkle. "And you got it."

I reared back involuntarily, knocking my head against the wall. My palms pricked. I felt my heart in places I shouldn't. "You're right."

"Of course. I'm Father Christmas. Or Santa, if that's what you'd rather call me."

After a breath, I made myself think rationally. Toy trucks weren't an uncommon childhood want. It could have been a lucky guess, the color an even luckier one.

"I even remember it had a decal of a clown-head on the left door," he continued.

And that sealed it for me. No more room for doubt. I had given alcohol to and spooned with the embodiment of Christmas himself, and there he was, still on my bed and available to me. There were so many things I wanted—and perhaps needed—to ask him.

"But why didn't I get that scooter when I was eight? I wanted it more than anything."

"Well, you were a bad boy that year. Remember what you did to your older brother, Billy?"

The name plucked a chord in me. I hadn't thought about Billy in quite some time. He'd been dead at least a decade, and it'd been fifteen years or more since I'd last spoken to him.

"He was with his girlfriend out in the yard. They were kissing. Billy's tongue was down her throat, and he had his back to you. You took advantage of that, but you shouldn't have pulled his pants down. It was the worst possible time, and you knew it."

I could only sputter.

"It was the most embarrassing moment of his life, and he remembered it until his dying day."

I managed to locate words and pull them up past my lips. "You—you saw that?"

He smiled a brown and yellow smile.

Long-forgotten Christmas memories washed over me, drowning out all other thoughts. The tingle I felt in my extremities when I woke up on Christmas morning. My favorite bow—a red velvet one my parents put atop gifts year after year. The spicy eggnog my great-uncle used to make. "My God," I said. "You made the world seem like a beautiful place. You really did."

"Well, that *was* my job back then."

Now that I'd found words, they started to pour out: "When I was a kid, I had no idea what real life was like, how dirty and ugly it was. But you kept me in a bubble that made my childhood seem like it was spent in a gingerbread house."

"I guess that's a good thing," he said.

"Yeah, a good thing…" I continued to look at Father Christmas, but my mind was not on his face or anything he was saying, provided he was saying anything at all. Rather, I thought about the litany of soul-sucking jobs I'd held. I thought about my disappointment with sex, myself, and humanity in general. Maybe I would feel better about such things had I not been shielded, had I known from the beginning there was no magic in the world, and that all things bright and beautiful had simply been imagined.

"Could I have another drink?" Santa asked.

I came back to myself. "What?"

He repeated the question, but I just closed my eyes, saw myself reach for and give Santa the bottle. He took it, and I walked to the dresser and removed one of my old yellowed undershirts, rolled it taut, turned it into a garrote and crept up behind him as he imbibed. I wrapped the shirt around his neck—wrapped it, tugged it and saw sugarplums dance in my head and smelled the faint aroma of hot bread pudding as his tongue protruded and his face turned blue.

Instead, I reared up, now on my knees on the bed. I flipped him over; his body was practically weightless. I yanked down his pants, mounted and penetrated him. Santa's response was to wrap spindly legs around my back and knead it with his hands. "Faster," he said.

A moment of shock, but if that was what the old man wanted, then I'd tear him apart, leave him coiled and bleeding on my bed. I sped up, plowing into his ass as though it weren't part of something human.

"Harder," he continued.

I didn't know how much faster and harder I could go. I considered seizing the knife I kept between the springboard and mattress. I considered slitting his throat with it, to see if that would get him off. At that moment, however, I detected a little of that old Christmas spirit in my cock and balls—that special tingle I hadn't experienced in almost thirty years. Suddenly, I felt connected not only to a man, but a rolling ball of power. My head was luminescent, like a bulb burning bright. My whole body felt like a present, being unwrapped by happy hands on Christmas morning. Nutmeg flowed with the blood in my veins, and my interior world seemed covered in tinsel, everything silver and gold, everything shimmering. In reality, I was inside Santa. In my mind, I was eight and sledding down the biggest and most snow-covered hill I could find.

When my young-self reached the bottom, my old-self came. Spurting semen felt cold, like a billion snowflakes shot from my cock into Santa. I imagined them coalescing inside him to form a troop of miniature snowmen that danced up and down the length of his gi tract. But the flakes were on the outside, too. They fell across the bedroom in waves, gathered on the bureau, the nightstand, the bed and our naked skin in thick tufts of white. I wanted to dig mitten-covered hands into the snow, to taste of it and make angels, but turned when I heard something jingle.

Santa stood over the bed; I hadn't seen him arise. Though nude, he wore his trademark bell-tipped hat at a jaunty angle. A ruddy glow brightened his cheeks; his belly looked almost jolly. Below it, a long, thin penis curved like a candy cane. Somehow, I knew it would taste of peppermint. As Santa stared at me—*into* me—a broad smile enlivened a face that appeared years younger.

"Not bad," he said, a twinkle in his eye. "But get on your belly, boy. It's time to call me Daddy."

The Christmas Turn-On

by
Edmund Colell

Edmund Colell *is a newcomer in the bizarro scene. I met him for the first time a couple weeks ago at BizarroCon. My first thought when I met him was: "This guy looks kind of like if Shaggy from Scooby Doo was a member of Guitar Wolf." But after hanging out with him for a while I realized that the comparison was way off because he didn't once try to solve a mystery while shooting flames from a guitar. Outside of his stories published through* Verbicide *and* LegumeMan Press, *I hadn't read much of his work before he pitched me this story idea. Christmas morning from the perspective of AA batteries? Where being used in children's toys is a battery's idea of having sex? Which makes Christmas morning the ultimate battery/toy orgy of the year? In my world, that sounds like a must read story!*

So toss your stocking stuffers aside—nobody likes those fucking stupid wax syrup sticks anyway—rip open some presents, slide some AAs into your new robot dog, and get ready to have some fun . . .

Bing Crosby's "White Christmas" tickles a wet dream out of a lithium battery named Double, who wakes up next to his sister-brother Discharge. While saying "his" would normally be silly because Double is intersexed like all batteries are, he and other batteries are okay with male words. Words are the least of his worries, because tomorrow morning is the biggest battery orgy of the year: Christmas! To humans, Christmas means money, toys, videogames, and all kinds of things people give to each other. The toys and videogames are the most important to Double, Discharge, and other batteries, because such children's delights are where batteries get their sex.

Double edges closer to Discharge to say something, but then takes a slide back. Both of their positive ends would be touching if he really tried to talk to Discharge, and despite being envious of people for being able to have better gay sex, Double is no gay battery. By frequency and the power of their orgasms, batteries have better straight sex than people.

After an hour, Double gets eager for talking again and bumps Discharge once to say, "Merry Christmas!"

Discharge bumps back. "Merry Christmas."

Double bumps twice: "I'm ready. You ready?"

"Yes, very ready."

"Me too," says Double, then he leans on Discharge for a bit to say, "But, I'm still a little bit nervous."

"So?" asks Discharge, throwing Double off.

Double rears back and leans on Discharge again. "I just hope I like the ones I'll be fucking. I never met any other batteries."

Discharge throws Double off again with a knock. "Stop doing that."

Double, getting a cold oily feeling from where Discharge knocked his body, doesn't speak to Discharge again and takes a moment to question his sexuality. His micro-eyes look around the room and see the other batteries sleeping in their packs. Sugar plums and bulging prods dance through their heads, Double thinks, as both sets of his glowing blue nipples swell with horny buzzing. He wipes his wet dream cum on the plastic above him and goes back to sleep.

In the morning, Double and Discharge wake up at the same time as big hands pick them up and rip apart their tiny cardboard box. Both of them tumble into one hand and wince as their pairs of same-parts bang into each other. Then fingers pluck them from the hand and hold them up for a short dizzying moment in the air before Double is flipped upside-down and loaded into a tight space with a strong spring-loaded prong reaching into his negative end while his positive end pushes into a knob. Then, as Discharge is laid down in a different slot and a plastic cover closes over them, the skin of another battery reaches over to touch Double's skin. "My name is Amp," says the other battery through his gentle spark-touch. Then, Amp's same words are made louder as a surge quivers through both of Double's ends. The prong teases the neg-end as it opens a little and leaks juices, then the prong plunges deep, pulls back a little, and plunges back in. The poz-end expands and reaches further and further until tickling a different wet spot and pushing into it. Then the hard plastic beneath them softens, becoming a wet, glossy, and fleshy bed. Double can now see everybody, all having grown fin-like limbs with long tentacle fingers. Pecs and breasts mold out of their bodies with hardening blue nipples.

To his left, Amp is stroking Double's chests with pretty blue electric arcs caressing the skin that say to him, "Relax a little. Touch me back."

Double smiles inside and gropes Amp's chests with his own electric tentacle-fingers. "Ah, that's better," he chuckles into Amp.

Suddenly, Double feels electric tendrils slide up both of his butt cracks. The same fingers grope and claw Double's body, making him shiver. "Plump and firm," whispers the battery behind Double. All the while, Double can feel that this battery is not lithium like Discharge and Amp, but something with a slightly weaker current. "I heard that," says the battery to that thought, "and what matters is that I know how to use it. Still, glad to take a piece like you. Name's Alka, and I expect you to moan it. Now."

Double feels a wide load of energy penetrate deep into his neg-end while his poz-end swells and thrusts harder against the current. His good feelings become so good that they begin to hurt. With tears welling inside of him, Double complies: "Uh-Alka. Alka. Hhh*Alka*!"

"That's right, and I own you and everyone else in my teddy-bed," says Alka, and then his tendrils claw deep into Amp's and Discharge's bodies as he penetrates them both and squeezes their nipples. Energy fills in and out of the three to the rhythm of Alka's tendril-lashings. Outside, the teddy bear holding them named Happy Companion Buddy Bear is being chased around wrapping paper and other new toys like pastel-colored talking Elder God Egg Stackers, a plush streptococcus peelable ball, and the hot new Japanese-imported toy set known as My First Unit 731, complete with battery slots for making the cries of P.O.W. test subjects while the wire-fed doctors experiment on them. A little curly-haired boy with a three-toothed grin is the child chasing the bear, laughing as the teddy bear makes long jumps and cartwheels around the boy's two sisters who whine about not being able to play with their battery-powered Hussy Huskies and Plastic Surgeon play sets with the boy being so obnoxious. Parents, aunts, uncles, and grandma all chug down convenience store big gulp cups full of brandy-loaded eggnog, laughing merrily at the sight and falling around with just as much merriment as their head-wound blood sprinkles their Santa hats.

"Oh god," Double moans as the moisture in his neg-end squeezes out acidic lubrication by the pint, "oh my god, this is just too much."

Alka spikes his tendrils and battery-teeth deeper into Double's body. "What was that, bitch?"

Double struggles to leave Alka's grip for Amp and Discharge, shouting "C'mon, we've had enough!"

Amp wraps his tendrils around Double and attempts to fill Double's ends with his own energy to block out Alka's. "Double," he says, "follow my energy beat. Let me get inside you, and you will get inside me."

Double then feels a calmer and more relaxed form of stimulation flow into him. The poz- and neg-ends still flow back and forth, but the tendril-play is less damaging and Double can hear himself think. Amp's many mouths kiss Double from one end to the other, cuddling him and stroking the pecs and breasts instead of squeezing them.

"What about Discharge?" Double asks.

"I have Discharge too," Amp says as Discharge joins in and feeds in and out of them both to make a threesome. "Don't worry. If we hold together then Alka can't exhaust us all. Our lovemaking will be safer."

Alka tightens his bonds and breaks the three out of the calmness. "Don't you fucking dare try to make this boring for me. C'mon, one at a time, I'm going to make you all *squeal*."

Double does his best to feel more toward Amp than toward Alka, failing to ignore the pounding and tinglebinding. As Double reaches orgasm, his limbs all flail about while his ends swell up like balloons. Outside, the little boy catches the teddy bear which has now started to spasm with its eyes rolling in the back of its head. All the grown-ups shout and scream about Happy Companion Buddy Bear being Satan himself. Scared and crying, the little boy smashes the bear against the floor several times, breaking its limbs and popping open the hatch on the batteries. On the boy's last upward swing, Double, Amp, Discharge, and Alka are flung from the bear's body. Double can't catch Discharge and Amp with his orgasm still ripping through him, yet watches Alka's tendrils catch both of them. Double's happy and tickly feelings then fizzle out as he flies through the air and lands in the Christmas tree. He tumbles down the branches loaded with pretty lights, shining bulb ornaments, and smiling cartoon characters, crashing and rolling from the bottom of the tree to find that the other three batteries are gone. *Amp*, he thinks while looking around the other toys and pulling all his parts back into his body, *just hold on. I'll find help. Alka's too dangerous, I won't let him take you or Discharge away.*

A moment later, Double finds a hussy husky bent forward in the corner behind the tree with her paw hovering over the single-battery slot under her skirt. Her makeup is smeared over a black eye and the bra under her fishnet shirt has torn wires. Double rolls up and places himself near her crotch, and with the force of will he lifts himself onto the slot, where the hussy husky creaks her paw forward to pull Double in and start using him to masturbate. "Please," Double says as sweaty warmth begins to rise in his body, "you need to help me."

The hussy husky opens her mouth, and with a Billie Holiday voice she says, "Tell me what you need me to do, hon."

Double tries to settle his breathing as he says, "I need you to help me look for some other batteries. They should be on the floor somewhere."

She stops masturbating and begins crawling on the floor and sniffing, bouncing her booty around with Double's body giving her wet tickles. All the grown-ups have taken the children away for the moment, having left during Double's carpet rolling in order to seek the comfort and protection of a preacher. "Do they please as well as you do, sugar?" she rasps.

Double projects the memory of Alka's surges and dominations through her wires, and she jumps with her hind legs quivering.

After a warm sigh she reaches back to stroke Double's body again, giggling, "Now that's how you offer a reward, sweetie." Then, as she sniffs around the Elder God Eggs, she says, "Tell me, what's your name? My real name is a big number so you can just call me Barkode."

"Double" is said through a short spark.

"Well Double, if we find these other batteries of yours and they're as good as you are, then I might have the best

Christmas ever." Barkode leaves the Elder God Eggs and sifts around pieces of wrapping paper discarded in various spots of floor, sniffing between short moans. Her paws turn over several layers, taking short breaks to rattle off pieces of scotch tape that stick to her fur. Then, the scent hits her nose: musky electric sweat. Over by an open battery package, she spots a large, breathing shell of wrapping paper. After she swats the paper aside she finds not a few batteries but a great wire-coated clump of them. Their skins slink and slough away from their bodies and their body parts squirm around their thrusting positives and negatives. Dean Martins' "Baby it's Cold Outside" hums through surround sound speakers, intermixed with the crackles and squishes of their lovemaking. "Mmm-mmm," she hums. "Looks like we found us a party."

Two spasms in Double's body pass through him, the warmer spasm for Amp and Discharge, and the colder spasm for Alka. He pulls both feelings into his middle as Barkode delivers him to the piled battery orgy by crawling on top of them. With the hatch still free in Barkode's crotch, Double feels tendrils reach up from the pile and caress his body, filling him with the many moans and grunts coming from each battery.

A blunt voice crawls over the other sounds and grabs Double. "That's right, sugar-knobs. You can't say no to Alka's lovin' for long."

Double's scream rumbles up through his body and knocks all the moaning and grunting away, pulling his own body into aches and burning feelings. "Where are Amp and Discharge? You have all you want, now give them back to me!"

"You already have them because I have you."

Barkode sticks more batteries in her ears and bites off plastic bits of her flesh to plug in even more, humping the pile. "Double, honey, you really are being a mood-killer," she says as she reaches into her crotch and tosses him out. As Double feels the last shock of a "No!" by Alka, he hears Barkode say, "Why don't you make yourself useful and go ask some of my sisters to join?"

Double comes to a rolling halt by the plastic doctors and P.O.W.s of My First Unit 731. One doctor tucks the colorful wires under his coat back between his legs and lifts Double up. The doctor strains to take him to a small operating table, knocking away tiny toy syringes and scalpels. He pushes a button and the dissected and diseased flesh on the Korean P.O.W. flips over to normal skin. The doctor holds Double above his head and says, "A beautiful discovery! We can now test a new weapon -- the gigantic hyper-sexualized battery!"

Other wire-fed doctors clap, one of them shouting, "Dr. Itoi, you are a genius!"

"*Nippon saikō no!*" shouts Dr. Itoi in response as he shakes his fist and struggles to catch Double thereafter. He then clears his throat and says, "My hypothesis is that if the patient receives an orgasm from the device, then the patient dies in the process as his heart fails and his breathing clips short from the pleasure of the act and the tearing in his groin muscles."

A second cheer cuts down as one doctor says, "But what makes you believe that this is a reliable process?"

Double attempts to escape but is thwarted. The dimpled ends of Dr. Itoi's grin curl above his surgical mask as he pops open the patient's side hatch and says, "We have the materials and the test subjects. Now we apply and observe."

Double's ends sting as he is stuffed into the slot. Once the patient turns on, however, he feels wiry whips flail and tear on his skin, and the first cry from his body sprouts through the patient's mouth.

"We're looking right at success, gentlemen! Is the feeling not better than Christmas cake in your bellies?"

"No!" Double's puppet shouts as both sets of Double's nipples feel themselves peel from his chests on the hands of the puppet. "I have friends who are in danger and need help!"

"Of course they are in danger," says Dr. Itoi, "them and all the other P.O.W. rats such as yourself." He then laughs and adds, "And we *are* helping them!" to an immediate clapping cheer.

"No, I could care less about them. I'm talking about the other batteries in that pile over there."

Dr. Itoi cocks an eyebrow. "So you are telling me that you make friends with batteries."

Double struggles against his jittering body as the sticky heat molds his skin. Trying to hold his new voice together from his gasps of pain and pleasure, he says, "No, I am the battery. I'd tell you about how it feels in here, but there isn't a lot of time. You need to get me over to that pile right now!"

Dr. Itoi leans over the patient-puppet and removes his mask to show his wide-toothed and moon-shaped grin, cooing, "And why should we?"

Double's pleading cuts short at that question, crossing sets of arms over both of his chests and feeling numb to the penetration and the whipping. With a sigh, he says, "I know you really want to be a bad guy. That's just fine. Just leave the power source of a ton of slutty batteries alone and forget about being able to hear screaming patients."

Dr. Itoi opens his massively-toothed mouth to smack his lips and lean closer to the patient-puppet. "But it's Christmas," he whispers. "You won't be the huge scientific discovery I was wishing for if everyone else gets to have batteries like you. I feel inferior enough just by being part of a *toy* version of Unit 731 that cannot even perform the Cherry Blossoms at Night without a toy version of California and toy airplanes. Please, just help me fulfill my Christmas wish."

Double's snark softens as he feels a bubble of sympathy float up through his body and pop into an idea. He holds onto the feeling as he slips back under the lashings. "You've taken credit for it, so just claim everything that ever gets done with the batteries. I mean really, who's going to stop you?"

Dr. Itoi's eyes roll to the top lids as he mouths enormous words and pokes at imaginary figures. After a second or so of that, he turns back and says, "You may be right, my bubble-bursting friend." Once he says that last word, the high curves of his grin droop down to the ground as his ears perk toward a collective of constricted barking noises as the other hussy huskies have begun to pile onto the batteries one after another, humping the mound and biting off their skins to stuff more electric-cum-greased batteries inside. "Oh hell no," he mutters, then clears his throat and gestures to the other doctors. "Yes, the experiment was a success. Now hurry, we must take all the other batteries from the pile!"

The other doctors whoop and cheer as they rush their patient-laden tables toward the pile in the same style as shopping carts being rushed just the night before. Some of them trip over and get their wheels caught in the wires leading into the bodies of the other doctors, especially those of Dr. Itoi. Soon Dr. Itoi crashes into the pile and Double spills out of the hatch. "We claim these resources for the glory of Japan!" he shouts. "You whorish dogs will have none!"

Brenda Lee's "Rockin Around the Christmas Tree" slides and taps into the air as the doctors load moist and writhing batteries onto each of their tables. The hussy huskies turn over to gyrate among the orgy and throw orgasm-induced kicks at the doctors as more of them try to take the batteries away from them. Double rolls around the pile in a circle, looking for the same brand as Amp and the same expiration date as himself and Discharge. At the first sight of discoloration, he pops his ends in place with another battery and reaches his tendrils out to stroke and tease the other's body. "I'm Double," he says, "are you Amp?"

"You can call me whatever you like," says the other in a moan as he throws his limbs around Double and leaks fluid from his positive end, "but you should save the touch for my tender bellybuttons."

Double forces himself off of him and ignores his own moistening neg-end, saying "Not Amp."

He then gets a rare glimpse of the expiration date on the soft belly of another one and reaches his body up to lick it, groping around the plush and the solid while saying, "Discharge, is that you?"

"Discharge? Sure, I'll discharge all over you if you keep doing that, just...oh god, don't stop."

Double drops off before that battery can pull him up with the others, and just as he does so he hears a crackling whirr as Happy Companion Buddy Bear crawls up to the pile with Dr. Itoi riding on his shoulder. "*Nippon saikō no!*" the doctor hollers as eye-rolling Buddy Bear swipes at the hussy huskies on top and tries to scoop some batteries into his mouth. Barkode snaps her mouth out to bite at Buddy Bear's nose and instead hits his mouth, the bite softening into a long and passionate electric kiss. Several other doctors have torn open the Elder God Eggs and aborted the greasy-skinned monster babies in order to stuff more batteries inside of them, and several others have taken giant scalpels from the Plastic Surgeon Playset to slice up the hussy huskies, stopping as soon as they realize that more wounds equal more penetration spots for batteries.

The pile begins to thin out with sinewy wires and tendrils and globs of acidic jissom still connecting them. Double rolls under the warm and sticky connections, seeing the busted bodies of batteries cracked from overheat and hurrying himself along to the thoughts that Amp and Discharge can become the same way. As he keeps asking them, another battery says, "Discharge? Fill me with that stuff!" and the next one says "I like going inter-brand too, sweetheart, but I don't know any Amp." Soon, however, he feels tendrils constrict him and stop his rolling. "You need to stop teasing me like that," says this battery, "Alka doesn't play that game."

Double fills with scattering panic as his tendrils reach up to knock away those of Alka, though Alka only takes Double's tendrils and sucks on them. "So my little bottom Double has decided he wants to play rough, too?" he says before filing his own tendrils down to thin needles and plugging them deep into Double's howling body, the ends pulling up and tearing along his skin while tongues lick around the wounds. "Bleed for me," he says, mounting Double and feeding the ends into each other next to all of the other batteries' connections to him. In a brief moment, Double notices that Alka's connections have become so thick and heated that Alka's own ends have begun to melt. "But go ahead, punch me back a little. Bite on my limbs." Double's body jerks into convulsions as he goes limp feeling another orgasm rippling through his body, fluid flowing from his wounds and his ends, and had he been human there would have also been blossoming tears. "C'mon, give me something new. I wasn't craving you for nothing."

In the midst of Double's overheating body, he seizes hold of a thought from the night before, from when he and Discharge were talking. "You want to try something new?" Double moans.

"Surprise me."

Double takes a burst of strength to twist his body around so that the same-ends match up. "You got it!" he barks, and soon thereafter Alka's body slows down to break the hurting connection between the opposite ends. Alka's melting poz-ends and neg-ends connect to the same ends of Double's. Double holds on tight and thrusts away, feeling both the pleasant warm of sex and the sour warm of self-satisfaction well up inside him. For added measure, he reaches several mouths to Alka's backside to lick both of his grainy assholes.

Alka twitches, his color beginning to drip off of his body. "Jesus," he groans, "how can you swing that way? It's just…it's just…" Alka falls out of the pile's interior with Double holding on. After he lands and Double continues to shag his life away, his body curls up and molds to mush among the other slaughtered batteries. Soon the other batteries are falling away, "Party foul" rippling through each one as their tendrils retract, their supple breasts and firm pecs mold back to flatness, and their aligned ends detach from each other in wet pops.

The other batteries roll away from each other, some in groups, some alone. Double rolls up to the solitary ones and interrogates them in the same way. "I've had enough discharge for this year's Christmas, thank you." "Amp is that one over there. Don't bother me, you bisexual freak." Double ignores that last part as he feels warmth well up inside him, and with a cheer-hearted boost of speed he rolls up and tackles Amp. "I thought we would lose each other!" he says with a kiss.

Amp giggles and reaches a small tendril up to rub Double's bellies. "Truth is that I had already kind of given up to Alka by the time you did that. A lot of batteries don't get to die in orgies as massive as that one, no matter how many power-sucking toys come under the tree."

Double sighs, saying, "I know, and I don't think I could find anyone who can fuck quite like Alka can, but…" he reaches a full limb over Amp and continues, "but that was Alka, and he just didn't care. I care about you."

Amp gropes up a mound of Double's flesh and gives it a kiss, then soon after says, "Wait, what about Discharge?"

Double feels the new warmth cool down as he takes his limb off of Amp and tugs him along with the ends of his tendrils. "Follow me, we need to find him!" He rolls faster and faster, questioning each and every fleeing battery while Amp catches the ones that slip away. Each and every answer, to Double's sinking hope, relates to discharge as electric current and not Discharge as the battery.

He then freezes at the loud sound of the front door opening and heavy feet walking into the house. "Shit!" he hisses at Amp. "We need to hide. Quick, let's get under the couch!" And the two of them roll to just a few feet near the couch before the footsteps land in the living room.

"There he is, Reverend Wallace," says a drawling man. "That's the demon bear we told you about. And lookit that, he's kissing that dog toy full on the mouth!"

"Lordy lordy," says Wallace as he picks up Buddy Bear and Barkode and pulls them apart, the slime of the other batteries trailing out of their mouths as the batteries fall. Wallace then looks toward the doctors lugging their egg sacks back on their gurneys, and walks over to the surge protector to disconnect them. With all of that done, he turns toward the man and sighs, "The devil just tried to make a lustful mockery of Christ's birthday. Mr. MacConaughey, the best thing for you to do is to take all these horrid toys and throw them in the garbage. Toss the batteries too."

"I'll never doubt your word, Reverend," says Mr. MacConaughey as he picks up the hussy huskies, the doctors and patients, the surgery set, and Buddy Bear to throw them all away. His son and his daughters whine and complain about each toy falling in the trash, but he shakes his head and goes, "We're getting you better toys than these. Stop your bitching."

Double and Amp stand still as Mr. MacConaughey begins to pick up handfuls of batteries. The two of them hug each other one more time and resume shape as another man enters from the opposite end of the room.

"Thank God I can snatch a few," whispers the man as he stuffs them into his pocket and pulls himself back up to his feet. With a frustrated drowsiness lingering in his head, the man thinks, *Uncle Ralph is going to need a whole lot of T.V. and booze to get through the rest of this holiday, and if I'm going to lose out on some free new remote batteries then my name isn't Uncle Ralph!*

"What's going on?" Amp asks, pulling closer to Double.

"I don't know," says Double, accepting Amp into his limbs. Then as the thought of Discharge dawns on him again, his comfort falls to pieces as he is left stroking Amp and feeling his own body turning numb. "I'm sorry, Discharge."

* * *

At the end of the night, Uncle Ralph is back at his own house, having helped his brother throw away the rest of the batteries and pick out new toys for the kids. In front of him sits a boxy television playing "It's A Wonderful Life." A twelve-pack sits next to him, depleting by one can for every half-hour. In his hand is an old remote, and in the old remote are Double and Amp.

Double runs several tongues along the length of Amp's body and pumps his body back and forth as the ends slide in and out of each other. This thought occurs to him: "You know, maybe Discharge will have a blast when he gets to the landfill. I'll bet there are many batteries there if so many humans throw them out."

Amp sucks on the tongues and rubs Double's back.

"Let him have them, as long as I can have you. Merry Christmas."

"Merry Christmas."

The ELF SLUT Sisters

by
Cameron Pierce
and
Kirsten Alene

Cameron Pierce *is one of the shining young stars of the bizarro genre and someone I have mentored since he was a teenager. I've seen him grow into a fine young man, one who physically assaults audience members in his readings by throwing pickles, hubcaps, or raw meat at them while wearing a banana suit and carrying a sword. His books, which I often call "Dr. Seuss meets David Cronenberg," have already become staples in the bizarro genre. From* The Pickled Apocalypse of Pancake Island, *about a sad pickle who falls in love with a beautiful pancake, to* The Ass Goblins of Auschwitz, *about children imprisoned within a concentration camp run by sadistic monsters called the ass goblins, Cameron's books are as cute and playful as they are surreal and disturbing.*

Kirsten Alene *was just published in the New Bizarro Author Series with her first book,* Love in the Time of Dinosaurs, *which is a tale of love, betrayal, and kung fu magic . . . Not to mention dinosaurs with fucking machine guns! Kirsten seems like such a nice girl in person, but I think Cameron must have corrupted her while co-writing this story because it is perhaps the most perverted and vile story in this book. It's elf porn, basically, a weird fucking elf porn story.*

So get into your reindeer pajamas, crawl into bed with a loved one, and enjoy the magical adventure of two adorable young elf sisters . . .

Betty and I were on our way to Daddy's house to spend the holidays with him when a blizzard practically wiped the highway off the map.

Betty is my twin sister. She's the tall, skinny one. I'm the short, fat one. Daddy calls us the two most fuckable cunts in this cold country. I think he just misses Mama, who succumbed to tuberculosis last year.

Now, we wouldn't have gotten so lost if Betty pulled over and let the storm pass. She's so impatient and stubborn, she kept on driving even though polar bears in this region are notorious for preying on stranded, nubile elves such as us.

"Betty," I told her, moments before she crashed the car into Santa's reindeer barn, "if Daddy don't give your anus an aneurism this Christmas, I'll tear my tits off and feed 'em to the penguins." Then we busted through the side of the barn and ran over poor Rudolph.

At first, we thought maybe we'd driven into one of those big factories where they farm reindeer for their meat and fur. Then Rudolph, that red-nosed son-of-a-bitch, started bleating like a baby seal getting raped by narwhals.

All at once, all the reindeer began to scream.

We tried to pry open the car doors, but Betty had done a pro job of wedging us in. We were trapped, two succulent elf sisters at the mercy of whoever found us.

A short while later, Santa Claus himself stumbled up to the car.

"Strike my loins, it's Santa," Betty said. "What great fortune to find, in such terrible circumstances, the jolliest man alive."

Betty and I had never met Santa before. Naturally, we were excited. He'd retired from the gift trade and become a recluse before we were born. Even the location of his ranch was a big secret, so crashing into Santa's reindeer barn in the middle of a blizzard was sort of like the best accidental Christmas present ever.

Betty cranked the window down and said, "We're terribly sorry, Mr. Claus. My sister and I were on the way to spend the holidays with our lonely widower father, but somehow we've wound up in your reindeer barn. We'll do anything to repay you for the damage. Honest. Anything."

Santa looked at us with green eyes that made my pussy wet.

Then he tore off the driver-side door with a gargantuan gloved hand, pushing me onto the tip of the orgasm iceberg. I have a thing for large hands.

He wiped some cookie crumbs out of his beard, winked at us, and turned to assist Rudolph.

Betty hopped out of the car and knelt beside Santa. She ripped her sweater down from its v-neck collar and pulled out her tits. She lowered herself to Rudolph so the reindeer could suckle, then she grabbed Santa by the back of the head and guided him to her other breast. She moaned as the reindeer and the old man nursed.

I witnessed the action through the windshield. Santa's mouth was big enough to suckle ten titties at once. The reindeer bucked on their leashes, anxious for elf milk. I was fuming with jealousy. Betty and I never fucked, let alone touched or sucked, any man, woman, child, or beast, without first agreeing on the job, and we *always* started together. This was a major betrayal on her part.

When her tits were deflated and empty of milk, Betty tore off her pants and grabbed Rudolph by the head. The reindeer was dead by this point, but she horn-fucked him anyway.

I looked at Santa, hoping he'd slap Betty for mistreating his poor dead animal, but an erection as big as a whale's burst through his red spandex pants.

He forced his cock into the reindeer's loose asshole. He must've worked Rudolph before.

It pleased me that Santa preferred a dead reindeer to my sister. I shoved a hand down my pants and focused on him. I was nearing my climax when Rudolph's broken jaw opened, forced wide by the purple head of Santa's cock. Betty bucked forward on the horns that must've been a foot deep in both her holes. The cock's head was bigger than hers, so she pulled a move I'd never seen in my life. Betty stuck her face in that great gaping pisshole and ate it out like we used to eat out Mama after Christmas dinner. Santa reached out and stroked her hair with the pinky of one of his gloved hands. Gently, he pushed her entire head into the pisshole.

At first Betty panicked, flailing her limbs and twisting on the horns enough to cause her pussy to bleed, and Betty's was an iron pussy. That furball never bled.

But with great tenderness, Santa guided Betty in the fine and formerly unknown art of head-fucking a pisshole.

I forgot all about my own attempts to orgasm until Santa and Betty came together. Then I yanked the car key from the ignition and ground the jagged metal teeth into my vulva, sawing the clitoris clean off. My scream distracted them from their fuckfest.

Betty pulled her head out of Santa's pisshole and slid off of Rudolph's horns. She hurried to the driver's side door and said, "Oh jeez, Mabel, what have you done to yourself?" Through the mask of semen coating her head and shoulders, I could see the look of guilt on Betty's face. I dangled my severed clitoris between two fingers.

Santa pushed Betty aside. "Ho ho ho, you didn't tell me you had a friend," he said. He reached one of his massive hands into the car and took my clitoris from me. He slurped it into his mouth like a string of spaghetti. When he pulled it out, the fleshy ball was clean of blood. "Sweet as mackerel pie," Santa said. He sucked my clitoris into his mouth again, holding it between his lips and gums like a wad of chewing tobacco. His eyes rolled back in his head. I had a spasm of delight, seeing the old man enjoy the meat of my loins.

But I was close to passing out from blood loss. "Santa," Betty said, in her candied little girl voice that she adopted whenever she wanted to ask a favor of a man, "my sister is deathly close to passing out from blood loss, and the blizzard out there is blowing something fierce. Is there any possible way we could dress her wounds and lie her down, at least until the storm lets up? Anywhere will do, even this musty old reindeer barn. We don't even have to spend the night."

"Sisters? Ho ho ho, and just when I thought I'd never get what I wanted for Christmas. I've never had sisters before."

"But what about on Christmas Eve?" Betty said, feigning concern.

Santa laughed a little shyly. "Oh, I've occasionally stumbled upon little girls sleeping in beds and tickled their truffles while they dreamed of me giving them presents, but I was only touching. I never gave them what I really wanted to give them, if you know what I mean. Mrs. Claus always said it would sully my reputation if a bunch of tweens and toddlers who were presumed to be virgins all got pregnant on Christmas Eve. It'd be inconvenient for me if nine months later they gave birth to jolly little children with white beards, plump bellies, and red cheeks. People trust you in the gift business not to fuck little girls."

"Well may we come in?" Betty asked sweetly as blood pooled in the passenger seat beneath me.

Santa licked his fat red lips, looking from Betty to me, from me to Betty. "It depends," he said.

"Depends? What does it depend on?" Betty said nervously. I could tell that she was afraid that Santa would send us back into the blizzard and what with me close to passing out, it would be totally up to her to ensure we didn't freeze to death.

"What kind of cookies are you willing to offer Santa?" Santa said.

Betty giggled. "My sister and I bake all sorts of cookies, anything you want, and we swear they'll be the sweetest you've ever tasted."

"So your sister's clit suggests. Well, I suppose I can put up two stranded elf sisters, but you have to promise that for my act of charity, you'll show me all the charity in the world."

"Anything for you Santa." Betty batted her long eyelashes. "Tell him, Mabel. Tell Santa you'll be a good little sex toy this Christmas."

Just as I opened my mouth to tell Santa the exact number of positions I've been fucked in (97, if you count the nostrils as separate holes) I must have passed out, because the next thing I remember is the warm fat of Santa's ample stomach pressing against my side as I was carried out into the cold, then a fragrant wash of warm air and the sound of a crackling fire.

I awoke naked on the stone hearth. I could hear Betty moaning in another room. I felt between my legs to check if I was still bleeding, I pulled something wet and soft from my pussy. I brought my hand to my face and sniffed. Cookie dough. They'd covered my pussy in snickerdoodle cookie dough.

I licked my hand, tasting cinnamon, sugar, blood, and my own fishiness. They'd spread a lot of cookie dough between my legs. I decided to save the rest for later.

I got up and stood by the fire, warming my backside, then I moved toward Betty's moans. I could hear the rhythmic slapping of gigantic balls against her ass, the grunts and hoots of Santa. Then I heard a shrill scream and the unmistakable sloppy sound of flesh tearing. This worried me. Betty took a dick better than anyone. On a good day, her asshole could accommodate two fists and a dick and be button-tight again in the morning.

I remember one time over dinner Daddy dared Betty to fuck Biff, the meanest, horniest bull anyone had ever seen. Biff belonged to the neighbors. They kept him locked in a pen with electric walls twenty-feet high because Biff was so mean he'd gore any male he could, and he was so horny he'd fuck any female, whether they let him or not, regardless of species. Well, Betty never took a bet lightly.

She excused herself from the dinner table and came out of her bedroom five minutes later, wearing the shortest, sexiest dress she owned.

"And just where do you think you're goin'?" Daddy asked Betty.

"I have a date with a bull," Betty said, and she marched right out of the house. Daddy and I scrambled after her.

We followed Betty cautiously as she crossed our property over to the electric pen of Biff. The voltage surging through that fence could kill a person, but Betty slipped between the thick wires like a salmon. Daddy called after her, demanding that she get back out of there immediately.

He was scared shitless, but not even the imminent death of his own daughter could compel him to climb into the pen with Biff. I held Daddy's hand, as much for his sake as for mine. Biff emerged from the barn, huge bouts of steam rising from his nostrils. Hoof to back, he stood ten feet tall. Betty kept her distance.

She looked scared but, after only a moment, she began to sway from side to side, her hips gyrating sensuously. Biff stamped his feet. Between his hind legs, a black dick stiffened and swelled. The bull seemed to smile but with animals it's hard to tell.

Betty continued to dance, running her long fingers up her own body. Daddy continued to shout. Finally, the bull charged, head lowered. He was going to gouge a horn through Betty before fucking her. Betty bent over and raised her ass into the air. I thought for sure Biff would stab a horn right through her anus. Instead, he skidded to a halt and stared, entranced by Betty's ass. He came up to her on delicate feet and proceeded to lick her ass with his long black tongue.

We had thought it was the end for Betty. Instead, she had the beast that had killed and raped so many eating out her ass.

Daddy began to cry. "Will you look at that," he said. "It's magic."

Betty farted once or twice, just to assert her power over the bull. After a while, she lay down beneath the bull and let him slather her in several gallons of hot cum. I know it was hot because steam rose off her flesh, and I saw the burns later that night, when I crawled into Betty's bed and asked if I could eat her ass too.

We'd fucked each other before then, but only casually. The night Betty tamed Biff was when our sisterhood definitively exploded into something beyond mere sexuality. It's when we decided that we would become elf goddesses of love. If something could be fucked, we'd fuck it, and we'd do it out of love for each other.

Entering the kitchen after I'd woken from a blackout caused by clitoral loss, Santa's cock usurped all notions of sex I had previously held. Betty was pinned facedown on the floor beneath the rollicking fat of Santa's belly. Betty's flesh bulged in places, as if snakes were crawling under her skin. It didn't take me long to realize they were the veins of Santa's penis. He'd literally filled her up. I worried about organ damage and broken bones, but if anyone could take a full-body cock colonic, it was Betty.

But instead of pride, I felt that Betty had betrayed me, again. Ever since Biff, we never fucked apart. It was true that Betty had always dreamed of screwing Santa, but that was every elf girl's dream. We dreamed that dream together.

Despite feeling like the third wheel, I cooed erotically to alert them to my presence, and jumped into the sexual fray. I sucked on Santa's toes, a minor pleasure compared to the full internal fucking Betty was taking from him, but minor pleasures should never be underestimated during sexual engagement. The slightest brush of a fingertip along a protruding notch of spine, a kiss behind the knee, the tickle of hair tossed across a shoulder, a nose pressed into the Adam's apple to plant a thought of strangulation . . . minor pleasures were my territory. I was the solitary snowflake to Betty's field of snowmen.

So I sucked on Santa's scabby toes. The gray cheese between those toes was more than I expected, but I accepted it gratefully. I tried to quell my jealousy of Betty, for without her I would not even have Santa's toe cheese. I sucked on the toes harder, tonguing beneath the nails more vigorously, yet nothing could ease the feeling of betrayal.

Maybe it had all been an act. Maybe Betty had always been waiting for the time when she could prove her superiority over me, waiting to dominate me, as she had dominated Biff. I felt suddenly disgusted.

If that were the case, then she would have to try harder. I was resolved to prove to her, by the time we left Santa's, that she needed me as much as, and perhaps even more than, I needed her.

For the moment, I closed my eyes and focused on sucking toes, until Santa let out an ecstatic wail and a tremor shivered down to his feet. I lifted my eyes and witnessed a fountain of sperm billow out of Betty's mouth. She was a glorious fountain. I wondered how it felt, a cock rubbing against your lungs and making your neck bulge out like a walrus's. When she caught me staring, Betty winked at me.

After the sexual encounter in the kitchen, Santa served us milk and snickerdoodle cookies in the room where I'd awoken. We sat around the fire, Santa and Betty glowing, and me, picking smelly toe grout from between my teeth. I asked them about the cookie dough smeared on my pussy.

"I'd planned to eat you out after you woke up, let you marinate a little," Santa said, "but your sister didn't want to wait. She overtook me and, being the gentleman that I am, I couldn't deny her a ride on the jolly stick." That's what Santa called his penis. The jolly stick. "I'd go down on you now if your sister hadn't sucked the last ounce of sexual energy from my enormous cock. Thanks for the toe kisses, though. They were sweet."

I took a long drink of milk to hide my disgust.

"What about your sister fetish?" Betty asked. "Wouldn't you still like to fuck both of us? Mabel and I have always fantasized about double-teaming you. It's a shame that my urges overcame me and we couldn't share you tonight, but Mabel likes big cocks too. Don't you, Mabel?"

I choked on the milk. Santa laughed, spraying cookie crumbs across the room. The cookie dough covering my crotch had grown crusty, and I was beginning to believe that this really was an elaborate plot of Betty's, meant to subdue and humiliate me.

Santa dipped two cookies in his milk and shoved both in his mouth at once. "You," he said to Betty, talking while he chewed, "are the greatest thing the jolly stick has ever plunged. Given the chance to fuck all the sisters in the world at once, any time I wanted, I would turn it down just to lay with you a single time. Unless your sister is as good as you, I don't think the jolly stick will feel inclined to plunge another pussy again. You have set my loins, and thus my heart, on fire. I'll be placing a call to Mrs. Claus in the morning to request that she never return from Nepal. You and I are to be married, sweet elf."

"Won't there be outrage over you leaving Mrs. Claus to marry an elf?" Betty asked, her eyes wide and reflective.

"Mrs. Claus was infertile. I'm an old man and if I don't impregnate something soon, my lineage will be lost forever. You'll bear me children, won't you, sweet elf?"

"It would be my honor," Betty said, "but I have one request."

"And what is that?"

"I want my sister to live with us. She's a wonderful cook. I'm sure she'd love nothing more than to be Santa's little chef, isn't that right sis?"

Rage boiled up within me. I tried to focus on the crusty toes tapping on the thick rug. The toes I had just sucked clean while my sister received the largest dick we'd ever encountered. I couldn't see any way that this situation could get worse until Santa shrugged and said, "I'm not looking for a chef, actually. I take great joy in cooking. Nobody prepares my meals for me. I do all the cooking around here."

Betty sank farther into Santa's corpulent breast and sighed.

"However, we do have a sort of a food crisis on hand."

Betty perked up, "Oh?" she cooed.

"I'd intended to eat Rudolph for dinner on Christmas, you see. He was getting up there in years and had trouble moving around. Since you ran over him and I fucked his body cavity, his meat's no good anymore. With Rudolph gone, I didn't know what to eat on Christmas, but you've given me an idea. How about I cook your sister? I've never eaten an elf before."

I opened my mouth to protest, but Betty interrupted. "That's a brilliant idea, Santa. Let's eat my sister!" She turned to me. "What do you say? We're always looking for ways to grow closer together. How about Santa and I eat you? It's like you'll always be a part of us and we'll always be a part of you."

"Except I'll be dead."

"Being dead is easy," Santa said. "Anyway, if you'd taken after your sister and learned to fuck like a champion, you wouldn't be in this situation."

"Who said I can't fuck like a champion?" I cried.

"Daddy did." Betty snapped, suddenly vicious.

"Daddy didn't say that!"

"Did too."

"You're a liar. Daddy always tells me I have the squishiest pussy of any elf." I blinked rapidly, trying to fight back the tears. I didn't want to cry in front of Betty, not now.

"Yeah, but Daddy likes his pussy firm. He told me on the phone last week that he tried fucking a block of tofu and it was useless. He had to stick a finger up his butt just to come. He said the tofu reminded him of you. He basically called your pussy worthless."

"He did not."

"Ho ho ho, cat fight! Break it up, girls. Santa's tired. I think we've reached a fair and final agreement here. Does anyone else have anything to add, or can we retire for the night?"

"I refuse to be anyone's Christmas dinner," I said.

"Ho ho ho, you should have thought of that before you ran over my favorite reindeer."

"I wasn't the one driving. My sister is a maniac on the road. She's the reason your reindeer is dead."

Santa smacked his lips and combed a hand through his

beard. He didn't seem to have heard me. "Come to think of it, I still haven't gotten the tang of your clitoris out of my mouth. If the rest of you is as delectable, you'll be a real Christmas treat, perhaps marinated in maple syrup and soy sauce."

"Why don't you fill her with your cum? I bet it'd bring out some real festive flavors," Betty said.

"Ho ho ho, Santa doesn't fuck his dinner, child. It's bedtime now. I'm much too old to stay up late on Christmas Eve anymore." Santa rose to his feet slowly and awkwardly.

"Can I sleep with you, Santa?" Betty asked, rubbing one bare breast up and down Santa's hairy leg.

"I'm afraid not. Until Mrs. Claus and I begin divorce proceedings, it's immoral to share my bed with you. Sleep out here by the fire. We're eating your sister tomorrow, so enjoy your final night with her." To me he said, "Don't try to escape. My bedroom is right here, so I can hear everything. My sleigh is out back and my reindeer are in top shape. If I find you gone in the morning, I will track you down and eat your heart while it's still beating." Then he chuckled, "Ho ho ho," and turned toward the hall.

"I'll keep an eye on her. Goodnight, Santa dear," Betty said. Santa waddled into his bedroom and shut the door behind him. Betty sighed and reached for the last snickerdoodle on the plate. She broke the cookie in half, giving half to me.

"What the fuck," I said, crumbling the cookie between my fingers.

"What the fuck yourself. I would have eaten that," she said, eying the cookie remnants on the rug.

"Like you'll eat me?"

"Oh come on, it's not that bad."

"Not that bad? This is the biggest fucking betrayal in the history of ever, and you know it."

Betty scowled into the fire. "Don't you realize what a great opportunity this is for me? If you loved me, you'd be happy."

"Happy about what? Happy that my own sister set me up to become Christmas dinner for a fat geriatric in a red suit?"

"Don't talk about my future husband that way. Besides, I set nothing up. Things just happened how they always happen."

"And how's that?"

"I'm fuckable, so I fuck. And you just leech off of the chemistry between me and my partner."

"I do not. I add…"

But Betty interrupted me, "Think about it, Mabel. When's the last time you got fucked really good?"

"Last night. You and I . . ."

"I'm your sister. Fucking me doesn't count."

"We do everything together, Betty."

"We did everything together, now I'm moving on. I don't understand why you can't just be happy for me." Her face was still slick and reflective with dried cum and the firelight flickered on her cheeks as she stared at me blankly.

"I thought we were close. I thought you loved me."

"I do love you," Betty said. "Digesting you and shitting you out will be erotic. You and me will never be closer than when you squeeze through my bowels. Go to sleep now. And be glad that life has worked out the way that it has."

Betty turned away from me and fell fast asleep, her face to the fire. I was devastated. True, I had known from the beginning that this was all a plot to humiliate and destroy me so that Betty could have everything to herself: Santa, Daddy, the bull, they were all the same to her - possessions. And she didn't want to share.

I had hoped. I'd hoped that I was mistaken, that this was just a joke or another one of her games. But then, who could blame her? With the loss of my clitoris, I would never feel the things we had felt together again. I was just a number of lifeless, dry, spongy orifices. I was no use to anyone.

Tears streamed down my cheeks. I hated Betty, I hated every inch of her, from her luscious fawn-colored locks to her slender white ankles. I didn't deserve to die. To be trumped, humiliated, ignored, and then eaten. I needed to escape, to brave the storms. I could find my way to Daddy's by myself. I might even be able to hijack a reindeer.

Gathering my courage, I stumbled to my feet. I crept toward the front door, willing the wooden floorboards not to creak. At last my fingers closed on the doorknob.

I pulled the door open. There was a loud snort. I jumped. As the porch light clicked on a menacing face peered in from the swirling blackness of the night. It was Prancer. He snorted again and took a step forward. His antlers were thick, enormous, like huge wooden webs blocking my escape. In desperation I grabbed hold of one antler and pulled down, smashing Prancer's face into the cold stone. With a sort of whine, he attempted to shake me off but I held on, braced myself against the frame of the door and pulled as hard as I could. The thousands of cocks I'd hand-fucked had given me tremendous upper body strength. With a mighty crack, the antler broke away from Prancer's skull and the reindeer collapsed in a pool of blood.

I stumbled back, dragging the antler. Out of the darkness beyond, other faces were materializing. Dasher, Dancer, Vixen, Comet, Cupid, Donder, and Blitzen. They were livid. Not only had we killed their most beloved company member, Rudolph, I had just stripped another of his reindeer manhood.

I slammed the door. Reindeer couldn't open doors. Or could they?

I turned the deadbolt, just in case.

From the other room I heard the creaking of a massive body shifting in bed. I couldn't wake Santa. And I couldn't let him know I'd just vandalized another reindeer.

I hid the antler in the coat closet, behind a big box of bondage gear.

Looking at my sister, curled up on the rug by the fire, I suddenly knew what I must do.

I went into the kitchen and searched through the drawers for the biggest knife. I found a cleaver large enough to butcher an elephant.

I held the cleaver behind my back and returned on tiptoes to the room where Betty slept. The logs on the fire snapped and crackled loudly, but they did not wake her. She was a heavy sleeper. I would have her head off before she so much as batted an eyelid.

I stood above her and raised the cleaver over my head, clutching the handle in both hands. For a second, I expected her to open her eyes and say, "What are you doing, sister? What's driven you to this? Don't you know it was all a joke? I love you more than anything. Did you really think I would eat you?" But of course she said no such thing. She remained fast asleep.

The cleaver fell heavily, silently into her neck. But it didn't cut the head off. Too much bone and muscle connected her head to the rest of her body. I worked the cleaver down a little further, then unstuck it from the gristle and tossed it aside.

I retraced my steps to the coat closet and snapped off a piece of the antler. Returning to Betty, I dropped to my knees and wedged my thumbs into the severed flesh along her neck. My hands slipped in the blood. I worked the tip of the antler up across her chin, prying the flesh away from the muscle.

I worked slowly, for I needed her face to be in good condition if my plan was to work. I knew that I couldn't fool Santa for long, but if I could convince him I was her just long enough for him to stick his cock in me, and then, if I could fuck as well as Betty, he'd make me his wife instead. Even if Santa ended up killing me, I'd at least get to fuck him before I died.

I worked Betty's face off the layer of muscle and shimmering bone. The eyes were the most difficult part. I punctured one of them and the fluid that came out of it made the job even tougher.

Finally, I raised her face to my face, and I put it on.

I felt the eyeholes and Betty's soft skin on my own face. It was still slick with Santa's dried cum.

Then a board creaked behind me. "Merry Christmas," said Santa Claus, "ho ho…ho."

He was looming over me, his eyes and mouth dark, gaping holes of shadow.

"It's not Christmas yet," I said.

"It's one past midnight," he replied, taking one step closer, "and I heard a clatter."

I opened my mouth to explain, hoping that Santa would fail to notice in the dying firelight that the sleeping body beside me was faceless. But Santa Claus interrupted me.

"I always hold off decorating the tree until Christmas day. But the problem is, I didn't chop down a tree this year. It's been so cold and this storm hasn't let up an hour since last week. But I'll tell you what," he stroked his beard and smacked his oily lips, "How would you like to help me decorate my beard?"

I wasn't sure whether or not he had noticed the body. But my throat was closing up, I realized what I had done. "I'm sorry," I whispered. "So sorry."

"Why, child!" Santa Claus said, stroking his beard and extending his enormous stomach. "There's nothing to be sorry for. One elf is the same as the next for a Christmas dinner and you've saved me having to do the deed myself. Come up from the floor now. I certainly underestimated you." Santa reached down and pulled me up by the elbow. Placing an enormous hand on either side of my face, he pulled Betty's face off of mine.

"That's much better now, isn't it? How would you like to be my wife?"

I couldn't believe my ears. Relief flooded my body and I almost fainted. Santa's huge, strong hands held me on my feet. "Really? Really?" I said.

"Tell me your name, sweet elf."

"It's…it's Mabel."

Santa smiled and chuckled, "Mabel. What a lovely name. Mabel, how would you like to hang ornaments from my beard?"

I nodded, wiping Betty's blood out of my eyes.

"Good little thing, now go into the kitchen and fetch the needle nose pliers and super glue. You'll find them in

THE ELF SLUT SISTERS

the drawer beneath the sink. Hurry along now."

I ran into the kitchen, not believing my luck, a wide smile spreading on my face. I was going to be Santa's wife. Finally. And we would eat Betty's miserable body for Christmas dinner. Oh, things really had worked out.

I rummaged for the pliers then skipped back into the sitting room and presented the pliers to Santa Claus.

"Now, let us think. Do you know what would make the most beautiful ornaments?"

I shook my head.

"Teeth."

"What?"

"Now, kneel down, Mabel, and pull out your sister's teeth." Santa said calmly.

With a little more relish than was probably appropriate, I yanked Betty's teeth out of her mouth, one by one. The first was hard, but after a few tries I twisted it in just the right way and it popped out into my hand.

When all of the teeth were lined up in a row on the rug, Santa said, "Now glue them in." So I glued the teeth into his beard. They did make beautiful ornaments, glimmering orange and red in the firelight.

Santa's eyes and mouth were still shadowy holes in his sweaty face. He licked his lips with a fat, purple tongue and said, "Now yours."

My stomach lurched.

"My teeth?"

"Yes, now yours," the fat man said.

I opened my mouth slowly and edged the pliers in. It was a small sacrifice and I didn't see any other choice. I pulled hard. A bolt of pain shot through my head, blinding me for a moment. The tooth didn't budge.

"I can't do it!" I cried out finally, dropping the pliers.

"Oh Mabel," Santa Claus moaned, "I'm disappointed. I thought you were stronger than this."

"I'm sorry."

"Well, perhaps you'd like me to pull them out for you?" Santa Claus said, standing up from the couch.

I started backing away, but tripped over Betty's faceless, toothless body and fell to the floor.

Santa was pulling on the fingers of his gloves. He took one glove off and threw it to the floor.

I screamed. Each of Santa's fingers was a penis, including the thumb, and each one was gnashing three rows of razor sharp teeth in my direction. Coming closer. Then the five penises crowded into my mouth, my lips tearing at the corners as their tiny razor mouths chewed the gums away from my teeth.

And I knew, in a while, my teeth would also glimmer in Santa's beard, indistinguishable from Betty's.

CHRISTMAS CRABS

BY

Kevin Shamel

Kevin Shamel *lives a couple hours north of me, just around the corner from my favorite beer and sausage company... so he's always worth visiting. A professional psychic healer with a ginger mohawk who makes zombie cat sock puppets for fun, Kevin fits perfectly in the bizarro writing community. He's the author of* Rotten Little Animals, *about talking animals who decide to make a snuff film, and the upcoming* Island of the Super People, *about anthropologists in the South Pacific studying a primitive tribe of super humans. Kevin's Christmas on Crack story is the only non-pornographic story in this collection. But when he pitched me this story I just had to take it. Basically, he wanted to write an absurd apocalyptic version of Christmas Vacation with giant flesh eating crabs that shoot lasers. How could I turn that down?*

So roast some chestnuts and sing Happy Birthday to Jesus, then get ready for some family Christmas cheer . . .

On Christmas Eve, Rudy dreamt that Santa was fucking his wife. Rudy watched them from inside the fireplace. Santa and Rainey were really going at it. He wanted to tell them to stop, but something like tweezers was pinching his tongue. It hurt, especially when he tried to talk. Rudy and Rainey's fifteen-year-old son Skipp came along and tossed a burning joint into the fireplace, setting Rudy on fire. The flames didn't hurt, but they obscured his vision.

Skipp and his older sister Staci danced around in a circle at the foot of the bed, clapping their hands. Santa yelled, "Ho ho ho!" when he came. Rainey told him that was *so cliché*, and she shot him with a laser beam from her fingertip, burning him to a fat crisp.

Rudy snapped awake. It was still dark outside. Rainey snored gently beside him. Santa was nowhere to be seen. Rudy crept downstairs, made coffee, and watched the sun come up. He anticipated the best Christmas ever, even better than the year before. When he plugged in the tree, it shone like the dawn outside. Piles of presents glimmered under its impressive lights. Rudy stared at the tree, anticipating the magical day to come.

Not long after his third cup of coffee, the family started straggling downstairs. More coffee was made, and Rainey handed out some pastries. It was perfect. Both sets of grandparents, the kids…just like Sixteen Candles without the dude named after a duck's dork. The best Christmas Day ever was about to unfold. He could barely contain his excitement. Even the fact that Staci's friend Belinda was coming over to be his daughter's vegan-compatriot and join the protest against his grand turkey and ham feast didn't faze him. There was squash for them. And stuffing.

While everyone was eating their breakfast and counting up the gifts under the tree, Rudy slipped away to the bedroom to check his bank account. His huge Christmas bonus was supposed to have been deposited the day before, and he'd checked a couple of times and it hadn't registered. He wanted to be sure it was there. It wasn't.

Rudy chalked it up to the holidays, and was certain it would all be settled by Monday. And by Monday, they'd be boarding the ship.

That's when the whole trip had to be paid in full—half of it coming from his big bonus. The other, non-refundable half had come from the landscaping and swimming pool fund. But along with the bonus, Rudy was pretty much guaranteed a promotion. He'd make up the lost yard-improvement money within six months. Just to be sure, he emailed a quick note to his boss, Andy. Rudy didn't really expect a reply, but he asked if everything had gone fine with the bonus, anyway. Then he went downstairs.

"There you are," said Rainey's mother, Julette. She had a big box on her enormous lap.

"Here, Rudy." Rainey handed him a package about the size of a shoebox. She held one that matched.

Everyone had presents in their hands.

When Rudy had his gift, everyone tore into theirs. Paper and ribbons flew. Boxes were snapped open. It was a glorious gift frenzy, and Rudy was very glad to have set up the camcorders on either side of the room so he didn't have to bother snapping shots of his frenetic family.

He worked at his own gift—shredding the paper and prying open the tough box beneath. He pulled out the heavy thing inside and flicked off its tissue paper wrapping. He held up his present to get a good look, just as everyone else in the room was doing with theirs.

It was cool in his hand. Like a stone.

It was about the size of a football.

It was a crab.

Everyone was holding a fat stone crab in their confused, cold hands.

"What the hell?" asked Skipp, looking around.

"We all got crabs!" Staci exclaimed.

"Rudy?" asked Rainey.

Rudy turned the crab over in his hands. He looked up at the bedheads around him doing the same. "I didn't do it. Who bought the crabs?"

No one fessed up.

Rainey's dad, Hector, went for more coffee, hacking his way to the kitchen. He left his crab on the couch. Rainey went and checked on the ham and turkey in the oven.

"Weird," said Rudy's mom, Lydia. She went for coffee too.

"Well, they're certainly ugly," said her husband, Gerald.

"Yeah," everyone agreed.

They all put the crabs down after a while.

Rudy said, "Hey, kids, why don't you each open another present?" He knew there was much more than crabs under the tree.

Skipp reached for the box containing his swimsuit. Staci held either a hockey mask or that red crystal ball she'd been talking about for months.

But when they opened them, inside there were gray

stone crabs. Just like the ones everyone had opened before.

"What's going on?" Staci asked. She searched the inside of the box and found a slip of paper at the bottom. On it was written, *Add water*. "Did anyone see this?" She held up the paper.

Everyone searched their boxes and found identical notes.

"Open more," said Rainey.

They did.

Everyone reached for a gift and tore it open. Everyone came up with more crabs.

They piled them on the floor in the center of the room.

"This is a joke," said Rainey.

Rudy was confused and growing angry. The coffee in his mug was cold. "Crabs?"

The kids each opened another gift. Crabs.

Panicked, everyone tore open more packages.

No matter the size of the box, inside it was a stone crab. The biggest was football-sized, and the smallest was about the size of a pack of cigarettes. The pile on the floor grew.

"What does this mean?" asked Lydia.

"Everyone's gettin' crabs for Christmas," said Skipp.

"The Assholes!" yelled Rudy. He ran for the door, pulling on boots and a coat on his way out.

"What?" the grandparents asked.

"The neighbors," Rainey explained, following her husband outside. She bumped into Staci's friend Belinda, who was coming up the steps.

"What's up?" Belinda asked Staci, who came hopping out the door, putting on shoes.

"Crabs."

"What?" Belinda followed.

Skipp joined them as they trudged to the neighbor's

house, where Rudy was pounding on the door and yelling for Brian and Marissa to come outside. Rainey stood shivering beside her husband.

They made it there just as Marissa opened the door.

"What?" she demanded. She was wearing sunglasses and a black kimono.

Brian appeared behind her, dressed exactly the same. Only his kimono was too short.

"Crabs!" Rudy yelled.

"What?" Brian shoved his way out the door, his kimono flapping in the wind and showing (hopefully) just how cold it was outside.

"You switched all our gifts with a bunch of crabs!"

"Look," the Asshole began.

"No, you look! I'm sick of you and your anti-Christmas campaign. You've been nothing but a Scrooge and Grinch since you moved in, and I will not stand for another moment of it. I don't know what you've got against Christmas Cheer, but I demand my family's gifts back. And you can come haul your pile of crabs home!" Rudy grew louder and louder.

Doors opened up and down the street. People poked their heads out.

Marissa came outside. She was holding a football-sized stone crab. "Is this what you're talking about?"

"Yes!" Rainey said. She reached for the crab.

"Have it." Marissa gave it to her. "We've got a pile of them too. Just unwrapped them. We were blaming each other until it degenerated into sex. Brian was about to put them in the tub and add water, like the notes say."

"What?" Rudy took the crab from his wife.

"Yeah," said Brian. "Every gift was replaced with a

crab. I thought she did it. You thought *we* did it to you?" He snatched the crab from Rudy.

Rudy said, "I, uh, well. I thought. Yeah. I thought you were messing with us."

"Well we weren't. Come on, how and *why* would we do that?"

Marissa snorted.

"Rudy," Rainey said, pulling on his arm.

Martin and Brad from across the street came over.

Brad said, "Are you guys talking about getting crabs?"

"Yeah," Rudy answered.

Brian handed the crab to Martin.

Martin showed it to Brad.

Brad gave it back to Brian and said, "We got these too. About ten of 'em."

From down the street, Mr. Jameson yelled, "Did you people get crabs for Christmas?"

Martin and Brad headed over to his house.

"Sorry," Rudy said.

"Whatever, Olen," Brian answered. He went back inside his house, pulling the kimono over his butt cheeks. He said, "*You're* the asshole."

Marissa agreed and sauntered inside behind her husband.

Rudy and his family went home.

The grandparents were cooking breakfast.

"Well?" Gerald asked.

"It wasn't the neighbors," answered Rudy. He sat on the couch. Even the smell of bacon wasn't rousing him from the funk he was falling into. He stared at the pile of crabs.

Belinda picked one up. "They're really detailed. Look

at those eye-stalks. And even though the claws and stuff are all smooshed up, they look real. These are cool. I wonder if I got crabs."

"You didn't open your gifts, yet?" Rainey asked her.

She shook her bald head. "Naw, my folks won't even be awake 'til noon. We'll open gifts later."

"Breakfast!" Lydia called from the kitchen. She and Julette started putting plates of steaming food on the table.

Rudy stayed on the couch, staring at the pile of crabs as everyone went to eat. Rainey came and sat beside him.

"What the hell?" he asked her.

"I don't know, Pookie. But come eat some breakfast. You know, mom's traditional squirrel cakes with marmalade…"

"Yeah. Okay." Rudy decided that no pile of crabs was going to ruin Christmas. Maybe after some food he'd be able to figure the whole thing out. He joined the table.

Staci and Belinda were eating figs and oats at the kitchen bar. Rudy wondered if they had anything to do with the crabs. He watched them as he forked bacon and squirrel cakes. They did not watch him.

"Rudy, what are your plans for today?" Rainey asked, brushing a strand of hair off her forehead.

He looked around at everyone who was looking at him. "Well. I. Well, there were things to do that were gifts. I had. There were clues. There were…you know, those crabs have kind of screwed things up." He ate bacon.

After a while Rudy said, "We're going to make snowmen in the backyard, maybe have a snowball fight, make snow angels, and then drink hot chocolate. With rum. And eat cookies. Then we're going to sing songs together, and roast chestnuts."

Everyone nodded and murmured agreement.

"What about the crabs?" Skipp asked.

His father answered, "We'll deal with them later."

Outside they made magnificent snowmen. Staci and Belinda made a glorious snowwoman. Even the grandparents got in on the action.

Rudy thought about the crabs, but wasn't upset by them. He figured he'd get to the bottom of the mystery soon enough. He planned to search the house for the missing gifts. And even if they were never found, the big gift couldn't be switched out for crab sculptures. The limo would arrive at six. That was in—he checked his watch—nine hours. A snowball hit him in the back of the head.

Inside, over hot chocolate, everyone wondered about the crabs. Rudy poured extra rum in his drink. Rainey took her mug to the bath with her.

"I think we should add water," Staci said.

Skipp and Belinda agreed. Hector coughed up something and swallowed it. Lydia made a face and tried to swallow her hot chocolate. Gerald wanted to add water to the crabs. So did Julette. Lydia agreed once she got the drink down.

Rudy didn't want to. He stared at the pile of crabs.

The cat slid past the pile and hissed at it.

Rudy said, "Let's all relax for a minute, put on some Christmas music and chill out, okay? I have to check on something upstairs."

He went and checked his email. No word. Rudy played three games of solitaire, listened to some Sheila E., and went back downstairs. He slipped past the grandparents, who sat snacking in the living room. Hector snored loudly. Gerald was talking over him to the women about ham-radio operators who disappeared after hearing some strange sound. Lydia rolled pie crust and whistled Christmas tunes. Julette ate a cookie sandwich.

Rudy slipped through the side door and found Skipp and Staci in the garage. Skipp was smoking.

"What the hell, Skipp?" Rudy took the cigarette from him.

"What, Dad? I smoke sometimes. Like when the grandparents are here. Or we all get crabs for Christmas."

"Yeah," Staci said, "So do I." She snatched at the cigarette.

Rudy held it over his head. He said, "Well that's bullshit, kids. You're too young to smoke." He took a drag and held it for a long time, finally letting a thick cloud of smoke crawl from his nostrils.

He hit the button to open the garage and strolled out, smoking. Staci and Skipp watched their dad walk away.

"Huh," Staci said. She dug in her purse for another cigarette.

Rudy walked across the street and down the path between two houses to the community park. He flipped the cigarette butt into the frozen fountain. He gazed at the houses across the skating pond, wondering how many families awoke to holiday adversity in the form of stone crabs. A few kids glided across the ice. Rudy thought he heard sleigh bells. He shook himself off, repeating his Merry Christmas Mantra out in the clean snowy air. Then he went home to get the celebrating back in swing.

He walked in the front door to find everyone but Rainey gathered in the living room watching *Rudolph the Red-Nosed Reindeer* on cable. Hector was snoring. There were snacks piled on the coffee table.

As Rudy closed the door, a deep boom shook the house. Everything rattled. The sound rumbled and passed.

"What the hell was that?" Staci shouted.

Car alarms went off outside.

"Turn on the news," Julette said. She stuffed a chocolate muffin in her mouth.

Skipp changed the channel.

...me just repeat, this seems to be a global situation. Everyone got crabs for Christmas this morning. We don't have many details, but similar stories are coming in from everywhere.

He changed the channel to a local one.

...was actually the third in a series of explosions that are rocking the metro area. Police and emergency personnel are advising everyone to stay home, and stay indoors. There is little information to be gathered at this time. We have crews attempting to make it to the sites, but they have so far been turned away. We'll bring you live coverage as it develops. Jennifer, back to you.

Okay, thanks, Rachel. So, in case you're just joining us, there have been explosions throughout the city. Police and other emergency personnel are responding to the situation. We are unsure if this is the work of terrorists, or if it is linked to the worldwide Christmas Crab phenomenon, or who is behind that.

Skipp changed the channel.

No one knows, Dianne. Did you get crabs? Sure you did. We all did. And how many of you have added water? Well, we've got a pool here, and about a hundred of those crabs that we gathered from audience members and our crew, and we're going to—

Staci asked, "What the hell, Dad?"

"I don't know, Stac."

The family watched the news. Car alarms still blared outside. Smoke billowed on the TV.

Rudy said, "I'll be right back."

He went upstairs to his bedroom and checked his email. There was a message from Andy.

Olen, I'm sorry to be the one to tell you that you're not getting that big bonus. Elise told me at the office X-mas party that she was the one who actually crunched all the numbers and lines for the Wilson and Wilson report. I believe her, too. She took me back to her place to go over her data and stuff. I sent the report to the Big Guys with her name on it. Sorry, Rudy. Guess you'll be stickin' around town for all that time off. And you can kiss your promotion goodbye. I guess that means I'll still be your boss when you get back. I've got to go meet Elise and give her the gift I picked up for her yesterday. She certainly deserves it, after all she's done. Adios, pardner.
—Andy.

"What?!" Rudy read it again. "Fucking Elise? Fucking Elise? He's fucking Elise!"

"Rudy?" Rainey called from the bathtub.

"Damnit," he said. "Damnit. Fucking Elise. That lying bitch! That. That. That."

"Rudy?"

Rudy panicked. How could he tell Rainey that he'd spent all the landscaping and pool money on half the cost of an around-the-world cruise that the family would not be taking? They wouldn't let them on the ship if they didn't have the money. Of course, he could write a check and hope it didn't bounce until they were too far out to sea to do anything about it. They could at least get half a cruise.

Maybe more if he stretched it out. And would the cruise line really kick the whole family off the ship? His huge Christmas surprise could *not* turn into another disaster. It had to work out. Had to.

In his panic, he wrongfully decided it might be a good idea to slip into the bath with Rainey, maybe rub her shoulders or wash her hair and break the news to her gently. He would need her in on it if they were going to pull it off. Rudy thought she was probably worried about the booming sounds. He figured he could slip the bad news in with sexiness and the info about the explosions.

Rudy unbuttoned his jeans and made his way to the bathroom. He tripped over his pants while trying to slip off his shoes and fell into a potted plant, which he knocked over on top of himself.

"Rudy?"

Wanting to somehow keep himself a surprise, Rudy didn't answer her. He kicked at his pants, shaking potting soil around the room. His shoe flipped off and smacked into the wall. He accidentally righted the plant.

"Rudy?" There were splashing sounds from the tub.

Rudy twisted his pants off and hopped to his feet. He dropped his underwear and crept to the bathroom door, pulling at his left sock with his right toes as he slowly turned the knob.

"Rudy?!" Rainey sounded frightened.

He wiped sweat from his face, deciding to come clean. "Yes. It's me."

"Can you come in here?" she asked.

"Uh. Yeah. I was gonna." He opened the door.

Rainey stood on the toilet, barely wrapped in a towel. There was a red and pink crab the size of a medium dog in the bathtub. It was snapping its pincers and skittering back and forth in the tub.

"What the hell?" Rudy asked.

The crab stopped skittering and leaned toward Rudy. It shuddered. It began to shake. A high-pitched squeal came from the tub, and the crab grew. Its eyestalks unfurled from atop the crab's body. Its eyes opened. It stopped moving.

"What is this?" Rudy said.

The crab flexed its claws. It gathered its legs under itself, like it was going to jump.

"Rudy!" Rainey shrieked. She held out her hands.

Rudy grabbed them and pulled her toward him.

The crab snapped a claw at Rainey as she flew past the tub. It caught her towel and shredded it as the couple tumbled out of the bathroom door, landing in a naked heap. The big crab sprang out of the tub and Rudy slammed the door shut with his foot.

"What the fuck?!" he screamed.

Rainey looked over at her husband. She said, "I took one of the crabs into the bath with me. You know, added water."

The crab charged the bathroom door, thudding against it in a clatter.

Rudy jumped up. "Grab clothes!" Snatching up his own, he ran for the stairs yelling, "Don't add water! Don't add water!"

Downstairs everyone was watching the news again. Rudy barreled into the room screaming, pulling on his pants and falling on his face. He got up to find no one looking at him.

Staci said, "Don't worry, Dad. No one's adding water." She pointed at the screen and Rudy heard what the newscaster was saying.

Again, do NOT add water. The crabs come alive, and grow. They are eating people. Do NOT add water. We don't know where they came from, or how this is happening, but keep the crabs away from water. Keep them out of the snow. Stay away from the ones that have come to life. We are being told that they grow quickly, to about the size of a typical loveseat. They are very dangerous. They are killing and eating people all over the world. We have reports of the crabs amassing and—hold on a moment please.

The woman on TV put her hand to her ear, listening.

She continued, *I've just been informed that once the crabs reach full growth, they seem to be sprout laser guns from one of their claws. Yes, laser guns. They are rampaging across cities everywhere, and apparently now shooting people with lasers.*

Rainey showed up.

"Mom! What's going on?" Staci hugged her.

"We've got to get that crab out of here," Rudy said.

There were shouts of, "Crab?!" and "What crab?"

Rainey grabbed her husband by the shoulders. "*We've* got to get out of here!"

"No way!" Rudy ran to the door, barring it with outstretched arms.

Skipp asked, "Dad, what the hell?"

An explosion boomed outside the house, bits of things pattered against the walls and windows. There were screams. The car alarms stopped.

"We are not letting some stupid crabs ruin Christmas!" He shook it off and settled down. Calmly, he said, "It's nearly time for dinner. Now, your mother worked very hard on cooking a ham and turkey, and they'll be done soon, right, Babe?" He looked to Rainey.

"What? Uh. Yeah. I guess. I mean, I put 'em in at seven. So. Couple hours."

"So we're gonna get that crab out of here and we're going to eat our Christmas dinner in," he checked his watch, "about two hours. Right?"

Rainey shrugged and went to her husband, taking his hands in hers. "Sure, okay."

"Okay." He went to the fireplace and grabbed a poker. "Skipp, get the swords from the den and come with me and your grandpas to fight the crab in the bathroom. Everyone else, maybe warm up some more cocoa. Or help Rainey with the cooking. I want to smell some pumpkin spice or apple pie!" Rudy charged up the stairs with Skipp and the old men in tow.

"I should call home," Belinda said.

"So did this thing have a laser?" Hector asked outside the bathroom door. He hefted one of the swords and coughed.

"No. But that was a while ago."

They could hear the crab in the bathroom, rustling over porcelain and splashing in the tub. It skittered and screeched. Rudy assumed it grew each time it did that. It could grow a laser at any moment.

He raised his poker and counted in a loud whisper, "One, two, three!"

Gerald opened the door and the other three rushed toward the crab, bludgeoning and screaming as they ran.

Hector's head disappeared in a flash of red light which erupted from the right claw of the tremendous crab that was backed up in the corner near the toilet. The old man's headless body was snatched up by the crab.

Skipp hacked off the laser claw in one screaming swipe of his sword. He brought the blade up as the crab's mouthparts snapped at his head, and jammed it straight into its nasty maw. Rudy bashed its eyes into scraggled, twitching worms and cracked most of its legs with three seconds of pure fury.

A flailing claw caught Gerald across the head as he rushed in, and the old man was tossed back into the bedroom in an unconscious heap.

Skipp tried to free the sword from his dead grandpa's fist as the crab smashed Hector into the walls and floor of the bathroom again and again, shrieking blindly around the blade shoved into its face.

Rudy hacked at the top of the crab's shell with the poker, cracking it. He pounded open a divot in the fleshy armor.

The crab shrieked and grew while it fought to survive—it went crazy, stinking of seawater and something putrid, hissing and screaming with its remaining barbed legs kicking madly.

Once Skipp had the sword, it was only a matter of two quick chops through the top of the crab's dented armor before it collapsed, a twitching mass of stringy guts and flopping, crusty limbs.

Rudy and his son fell back into the bedroom, slicking guts, blood, and slime off of themselves as they struggled to stand.

Staci and Belinda stood in the doorway.

"Holy shit!" Staci yelled, "That thing killed Grandpa Hector!"

Hector's body, with its cauterized neck, was still flopping around in the mess of twitching giant crab.

Belinda barfed into her hands. The girls backed away from the door, crying.

Rudy went to Gerald. The old man came around after a few slaps. He was soon on his feet.

Everyone stumbled downstairs.

Rainey poked her head around the corner. She had a tray of rolls in her hands. "How did it go?"

Rudy shook his gory head. "Rainey. We lost your dad."

"Oh, no," she said. She nearly dropped the rolls.

Julette cried from around the corner, "Hector? Hector?"

Skipp took the baking sheet from his mom and put the rolls in the oven. Staci hugged her crying grandma.

Belinda ran to the bathroom, dripping vomit.

"Not Dad," Rainey said. She held onto Rudy.

"He saved us," Rudy said. "How long until the meat's ready?"

Rainey choked back tears, "Any time, really. We're waiting for rolls and mom's mashing the potatoes. Right, mom?"

"Not anymore I'm not! You take me to Hector!" the old woman screamed at Rudy.

"I'll take you, Grandma," Staci said. She went with Julette upstairs.

Belinda came out of the bathroom with clean hands and face and said, "Fuck this, I'm outta here." She went to the door, snatching her coat from the rack and pulling it on.

Skipp yelled, "No, Belinda, there's crabs out there!"

She opened the door and ran outside. Skipp, Rudy, and Rainey followed. Gerald sat down and fell asleep in front of the TV. Lydia was making apple pie and just couldn't stop.

"Wait!" Skipp called. He didn't want Belinda getting

killed. He was secretly in love with her.

Belinda stalked down the driveway. "I'm going home!" she yelled.

"We were just about to watch home movies from past Christmases!" Rudy told her.

"You're crazy!" she said.

The Asshole's door opened just then and Brian came staggering outside.

He looked over at the group in the driveway and said, "Don't add water." He slumped to the ground face-first, his sunglasses skittering across the icy drive. Everyone could see that his back had been torn open nearly to his front. Blood shot from his heart in gouts, staining the snow.

Two crabs leapt from the Asshole's open door, shrieking and scampering toward the people standing in the drive.

A laser beam streaked through the air and hit Belinda in the chest. Blackened, singed down puffed into the air. Belinda flew backward and tumbled through the snow. She sighed, "Fuck you," and died.

"No!" Skipp shouted, running toward the smoking girl.

His dad snatched him by the collar and hauled him toward the house as one crab grabbed Brian in both claws and pulled him apart over its mouth, sucking his guts loudly, and the other raced for Belinda.

Rudy and Rainey hauled their son through the door and slammed it behind them.

Staci came down the stairs. "Where's Belinda?"

"She went home," Rudy told her. "It's time for ice skating. Where's your grandma?"

"Ice skating? She's up in your room, crying about grandpa. What exactly happened to his head?"

"Laser," Skipp panted. "Just poofed it away."

"Everyone get your gear, we're going skating in the park. Staci, get your grandma."

"But what about dinner, honey?" Rainey frowned.

"It'll be perfect timing. We've got over an hour. Let's put the pies in the oven, get some foil on those rolls, and skate!" He herded his nearest family members toward the coat rack in the foyer.

Lydia put pies in the oven and wrapped up the rolls. "I'm not skating on a pond!" she yelled. Under her breath, she said, "That's how people die."

Skipp said, "Dad. Skating? There's giant crabs running around out there. With lasers."

"That's true, son. So get the shotguns."

Skipp ran upstairs.

While the family put on coats and retrieved the ice skates Rudy had so carefully packaged for each of them, Skipp and his sister returned with Julette.

The wailing grandma said, "I'm not going skating! Hector is dead! DEAD!" She sat on the stairs and cried.

Skipp handed his dad a shotgun. He unslung a bag from his back. "There's hundreds of shells, Dad."

"I was gonna shoot a lot of ducks, Skipp." He loaded the shotgun, nodding at his son to do the same with his. "Julette, you're going. Grab your skates. They're in that box there that says, *Hector and Julette's Skates.*"

The old lady cried harder.

"Daaaad," Staci said.

"Put as many shells in your pockets as you can, Skipp," Rudy said, stuffing his own pockets full. "Let's go, everyone. Julette! Get your coat. Staci, help your grandma, will ya?" He hung his skates from his neck as he had everyone else's and pushed his family out the door.

They huddled in the driveway, Rudy waved his shotgun toward the street. There were no people visible outside. Something exploded far away. Glass tinkered a few doors down. Snow was gently falling.

Skipp pointed his gun at the Assholes' house. He whispered, "Dad, where's the bodies?"

Julette staggered outside, barely supported by her granddaughter. She was dressed in a black coat and wore a white hat. She carried her skates.

Staci let her go when they reached the crowd. She pointed at the yard. "What's all this blood from?"

"Crabs," said Skipp.

Lydia said, "I'm not skating. Can't I just go back and check on the pies?"

"You're skating, Mom," Rudy said. "Come on, everyone." He led the shuffling crowd arm-in-arm across the street and down the path to the park.

Scuffling sounds inside the Merced's house startled them as they passed. Wood cracked, and things thudded on the floor. The group hurried down the path, still in a tight group.

Skipp craned to see inside the window as they passed, but only saw shadows.

"Dad?" he asked.

"Keep moving," Rudy said.

He led them into the park, past the frozen fountain, and to the edge of the pond.

"Where's mom?" he asked, when he looked over the group.

Everyone looked around and shook their heads. They sat and started putting on their skates. Except Julette. She said, "What, there's no bench?"

Gerald said, "You know your mother. She probably went back to check on the pies when we weren't looking."

"When weren't we looking?" Rudy asked.

His father shrugged.

"Okay," Rudy said. He sat in the snow with his shotgun over his knees and put on his skates. The snow gently fell. He felt pretty good, despite his mother sneaking off. Her fear of frozen ponds really bothered him sometimes.

"Dad, what's that?" Staci asked, pointing at the playground.

"Crab!" yelled Skipp. He jumped up onto his skates, though he hadn't tied the left one.

The crab skittered around the jungle gym/slide thing. Its claws clacked.

"Let's get it, Skipp," Rudy said, creeping forward through the snow.

"We should just get out of here," Rainey said.

Julette, Gerald, and Staci agreed.

"Shhhhhh!" Rudy said. He motioned for Skipp to follow him.

When they were twenty feet from the giant crab's hiding place, they could see its legs through the tunnels and gaps in the gym. It shuffled back and forth, clacking its enormous claws.

Rudy motioned for Skipp to go around one side of the equipment, and he crept around the other.

An eye-stalk shot out from around the slide. Rudy hefted his gun and fired—shattering plastic, wood, and crab-eye into bloody spray. The crab screeched and jumped backward into the air. Rudy could hear his family yelling from the pond's edge. He ran toward the crab.

Skipp fired as the monstrosity flew toward him screeching and snapping its claws. A laser beam arced through the air, slicing the swingset to the ground, melting snow in a wide line, and burning into a house behind the park. The crab's guts exploded as buckshot punched through its belly and blew out its armored back.

A snapping mass of stringy guts and claws landed on the boy, knocking him to the ground. He fired the shotgun again as he fell, blasting more of the crab, including its mouthparts and remaining eye into pulp. The crab pinned Skipp to the snow, twitching and flopping.

Rudy arrived, kicking at the thing with his ice skates. He finally lifted a tangle of legs and guts off Skipp, and dragged him clear of the mess.

They gathered themselves by the merry-go-round.

Rudy wiped some of the gore from his son's coat and face. "There," he said, "There. Better? All good?"

"I lost a skate," Skipp said. "It's in the crab."

"Oh. Well, you can skate on just one, right?"

"Well, yeah. But my foot's wet, and gettin' cold."

"You'll be fine."

Rudy helped Skipp up. They went back to the pond and joined the others. Skipp hopped.

"Let's go back," Julette said when they got there.

"Not until we've skated," Rudy answered cheerily. "Let's go! Skipp, you should probably put a boot on your other foot."

"Are you two okay?" Rainey asked.

"We should go home," Staci said. But she hopped onto the ice.

"We're fine," Rudy said, wiping at Skipp's coat. "Right, Skipp?"

"Yeah," Skipp said, slipping his frozen foot into a boot.

Gerald helped Julette onto the ice.

Soon everyone was skating.

Julette surprised everyone but Rainey by being an excellent skater. She did some leaps and stuff—reminding Rudy of the time he took the family to SeaWorld.

Skipp skated a wide circle around the group, keeping an eye out for crabs. He saw some kids go to the playground and run away screaming.

Rudy watched his dad slip and fall about twenty times. Rainey tried to help him up for the first few minutes, but finally crawled away, pretending to look for an earring as he rolled around calling for help.

He saw Julette doing some crazy backward skating maneuvers while Staci followed after her. They whizzed past him and he spun to watch them.

Rudy and Skipp noticed the crabs at the same time.

Three of them.

They skittered and slid across the pond, heading straight for the family.

Pieces of children dropped from their claws as they approached, skidding across the ice, leaving bloody trails.

"Crabs!" Skipp yelled. He raced from the far side of the pond, hoisting his gun.

"Crabs!" Rudy yelled, pointing behind Julette and Staci.

Staci stopped, staring at the approaching crustaceans. "Shit, Grandma, crabs!" She pointed.

A laser beam shot from the crab on their left. It grazed across the surface of the pond. The beam zig-zagged back and forth, cutting the ice and opening a gap between the crabs and the backward-skating Julette.

Julette said, "What?"

She turned just in time to notice she was plunging into

the water, and that three crabs skittered to a stop at the edge of the ice on the other side of a freshly lasered gap in the frozen part of the pond. Juliette dropped into the water with a huge splash and a birdlike screech.

Staci stopped as she watched two of the crabs pick her grandma from the pond and pull her apart as she blubbered for breath. Blood erupted from tears in her big body, spraying the crabs and splashing into the pond.

The third crab leapt the gap. It landed poorly, and slid onto its side, careening across the ice.

Skipp hop-skated full speed toward it, unloading both barrels of the shotgun as the crab staggered to its pointy feet and scuttled at his sister.

The crab's legs were blown out from under it and it was plastered in the side with heavy shot. It slid past Staci and splashed into the pond.

Staci turned and skated to her brother, who was reloading.

The other two crabs ate their grandma, stuffing her into their chittering maws.

Rudy called, "Come the fuck on, kids!" He was at the edge of the pond, off the ice, waving at them.

Rainy and Gerald were running toward the fountain.

Crabs poured over the fence near the pond.

"Holy fuckin' shit!" Staci yelled, pulling at Skipp. "Let's fucking go!"

They sped across the pond as the crabs hit the ice. They met up with the family at the fountain, and all ran down the path toward home.

Between the houses, near the tall hedges that bordered part of the path, they found Lydia's skates. And her hat. They were soaked in blood. No one stopped to investigate.

CHRISTMAS CRABS

They clattered down the path in their skates.

A car drove across their lawn in front of them as they crossed the street. It went straight across their driveway, bounding up and over the Assholes' yard, and smashed into a tree two doors down. No one seemed to be in it.

Rudy ushered everyone inside the house and slammed the door behind them.

They crumpled into a heap in the living room, panting and pulling off their skates.

It smelled like apple pie and ham in the house.

"I don't know about anyone else, but I sure am hungry," Rudy said.

"Lydia?" Gerald called.

"Rudy, my mom," Rainey gasped, reaching up for him.

He helped her up from the couch and hugged her. "I know. I know. I'm sorry it was your mom that had to die, and mine who came back to make sure the pies didn't burn."

Staci went into the kitchen. "Gramma?" she asked.

Everyone followed.

Lydia was not in the kitchen. The pies were in the oven.

Rainey said, "Oh, I should take those out."

"Lydia?" Gerald called loudly.

"Mom?" Rudy shouted. "Check the toilet, Dad," he said.

It was quickly surmised that Lydia didn't make it home.

Rudy said, "At least we have the pies. We should get cleaned up and eat."

"Well, I *am* really hungry," Staci said.

"Me, too," said Skipp, laying his shotgun across the counter.

"We really shouldn't waste all this food, and if we don't

get to it soon, it's going to be ruined," Rainey said.

Gerald moaned, "Lydia would have wanted it this way."

"Okay," Rudy said, "If you girls would get the dinner together, we'll block all the windows and doors. I think I could start up some home movies. I'll turn it up real loud so you can be sure to hear. Let's clean up and get to feasting!"

Everyone scattered to various doors and windows, blocking them off with furniture. Then they all found sinks to get clean. Crabs swept past the house now and then, and sometimes skittered across the roof. They seemed to be busy chasing people and cars down the street, mostly ignoring the house.

Rudy made a phone call and wrote an email to Andy, hoping he got some crabs for Christmas and wishing him a happy New Year. Then he washed his hands and face and went back to the living room.

He put in the Olen Christmas DVD but left the TV on the news for a moment, watching scenes of crab armies marching through cities and towns. The reporter was talking about the military's failing effort to control the crabs. He said that more and more crabs were coming to life, and that they were growing even bigger. The picture was scratchy and the newscaster's voice wavered in and out. Rudy turned it to the DVD when Skipp wondered aloud how many more shotgun shells they had.

Rudy heard a rustling sound and looked over to the fireplace. The cat was hiding under the tree. He figured she must have made the noise, batting at ornaments. He let his gaze wander, and noticed that the stockings hanging from the mantle were still full of gifts. He could see candy sticking out of Staci's.

"Kids!" he exclaimed. "There's stocking stuffers!"

CHRISTMAS CRABS

He leapt up and pulled down all the stockings. Everyone's stocking was there, packed tight with gifts.

"Come see!"

Staci and Rainey came in. The kids dumped their stockings out.

"Sweet! Lizard Zombie Apocalypse III!" Skipp shouted.

"Nice, thanks guys," said Staci, pocketing gift cards, clasping jewelry, and replacing the candy.

There was a scuffling sound near the fireplace again.

The fire went out. Gas continued to pour out of its burners.

Thin, barbed legs swept out of the chimney, followed by black eyes on stalks. A tremendous claw snaked its way out.

"Fuck!" Rainey yelled. She snatched up Skipp's shotgun that was leaning against the couch, snapped it closed, and blasted at the crab.

She hit one of its eyes, and all of its exposed legs. Bricks fell. Dust exploded into the room. The crab screamed, falling into the room in a hail of masonry and blood. Rainey pulled the second trigger.

The blast hit the charging crab straight in its mouth, driving it back into the pile of bricks. It flopped onto its back, and struggled to flip itself over—kicking at the tilted Christmas tree. It hooked a string of lights in its claw and fired its laser. A blast shot through the ceiling, burning a hole through two floors and the attic roof. The laser beam severed the string of lights, and the resulting spark set off the cloud of gas pouring into the living room.

Something slightly less than an explosion filled the room with just under a second of fire. It crisped the flailing crab, and knocked everyone backward.

The scampering crab righted itself as the fireplace went back to burning like a comfortable log fire. Rudy blasted the crab, splitting it in half and splattering the wall with blood.

Guts sizzled in the fire and on the tree.

The crab kicked and died. It kicked some more.

The living room and everything in it was singed. All bore a black patina.

Rudy coughed. "Well. I'm glad we got those stockings off the mantle before it was torn apart."

Everyone agreed.

Skipp righted the TV. It seemed to work. He started the DVD again.

Bricks fell on the mangled crab corpse.

Rudy shut off the gas to the fireplace and unplugged the tree. He kicked at the crab. "Stupid jerk," he said.

On the screen, Christmas music played in the living room. The second best tree in of all time was crammed in the very same corner of the living room where the blackened tree, covered in crab guts, stood now, and all the family was gathered around it. The grandparents were mostly asleep, and a slightly smaller Skipp was running around, tickling them.

Off the screen, Rudy sat down with Skipp and Gerald on the couch. Rainey and Staci went back to putting food on the table. The old man asked why he didn't have a shotgun. Skipp shrugged. They watched the DVD of their previous Christmas. It seemed pretty boring.

"I wish I'd have gotten that new phone," Skipp said.

"Oh, you totally did," Rudy told him.

"Damn."

"Yeah."

"Fucking crabs."

"Got a smoke?"

"Rudy!" Gerald said, "You don't smoke."

"Shut up and watch last year, Dad."

Rudy and Skipp went to the garage.

When they came back, the table was filled with food. Gerald was asleep on the couch.

"Let's just let him sleep," Rudy said. "He's had a big day for an old guy."

Outside, more explosions rocked the house. Something landed on the roof with a thud.

Rainey called them to dinner.

On the TV, she did the same.

Rudy stood at the head of the table and carved the turkey and ham.

Skipp sat facing out the window. He noticed the Assholes' house was on fire.

Staci looked up at her dad. She said, "This is all so gross. I'm not eating. Skipp still has crab guts in his hair."

"Do not."

"You do too, you fucking gimp. Learn how to wash."

"Are you kidding? We're all covered in crab-soot."

She stuck her tongue out at him. It looked very pink against her blackened lips.

Rudy put a piece of turkey on her plate.

Rainey said, "Ruuuuudy."

"It's Christmas," he said.

A limousine crashed through the living room. It broke through the wall, scattering pieces of building material, ornamentation, and furniture. The TV flew into the still-sleeping Gerald and crushed him to death. Two plywood candy canes still lit with Christmas lights whipped through the room like shuriken and stuck in the wall above the table—blinking.

A chair tumbled across the dining room, wiping out everyone's plates, and nearly taking off Rudy's head. He dodged the chair and smiled triumphantly at the car rocking in the settling dust.

The cat sprang from under the tree remains, bounded over the long trunk of the car, and launched from its TV antenna, soaring through the hole left by the car, and into the snow. They heard the cat hiss as she ran off.

Rudy gathered up his family as they staggered from around the shattered table. "Kids, Rainey, I've got a very special Christmas surprise for you." He walked them toward the limo.

The driver got out smiling and opened the door for them, kicking aside some couch cushions and bricks. Crabs clamored to get into the hole in the wall, but the car blocked them. They tore at the wall and the limo, screaming. A laser beam blasted into the chandelier, dropping it onto the table in a burst of sparks.

More crabs gathered in the yard. They scratched at the walls and crowded around the hole, picking at drywall and brick. Lasers started blasting through the room, cutting the walls to pieces and knocking chunks of the ceiling free.

Rudy helped his family into the car. He tossed the shotguns in to Skipp. Rudy paused before he got in and said to the driver, "Thanks for coming early!"

"No problem, Mr. Olen. I wasn't doing anything but driving around avoiding these giant crabs, anyway. I was glad to get your call."

Something exploded upstairs.

Dust and smoke billowed through the room. The lasers made it look like a disco.

The happy driver closed the door, scrambled over the hood, and got in the car.

He drove into the crabs trying to get into the house, smiling back at the family. The crabs beat at the limo as it smashed into them. The car pinned one crab against a tree and crushed it. Another aimed its laser at them, but the driver peeled out straight for the huge crustacean, and it jumped into the air, firing crazily into the Asshole's burning house. Other crabs scampered into the house, eating Gerald, the ham, and the turkey.

The limo driver announced, "Merry Christmas, Olen family! Welcome to your vacation. First stop, the airport. I hope you have a wonderful trip."

Rudy smiled at the driver and then to his family. "I'm sure we will," he said, "I'm sure we will."

Rainey smiled tentatively.

"Kids," Rudy asked, his eyes focused far away in some fantastic future, "what do you think about a cruise around the world?"

Skipp and Staci shrugged at each other.

"Oh, Rudy," Rainey said.

The Olens watched out the windows. Laser bursts lit the air around them. Crabs slid across the ice, chasing down families and eating them.

Rudy poured a hot chocolate and rum from the bar for everyone. He looked adoringly at his bedraggled family.

"Merry Christmas," he told them.

They raised their mugs in a toast.

ABOUT THE EDITOR

Carlton Mellick III is one of the leading authors in the new *Bizarro* genre uprising. Since 2001, his surreal counterculture novels have drawn an international cult following despite the fact that they have been shunned by most libraries and corporate bookstores. He lives in Portland, OR, the bizarro fiction mecca.

Visit him online at **www.carltonmellick.com**

Bizarro books

| CATALOG | SPRING 2010 |

Bizarro Books publishes under the following imprints:

www.rawdogscreamingpress.com

www.eraserheadpress.com

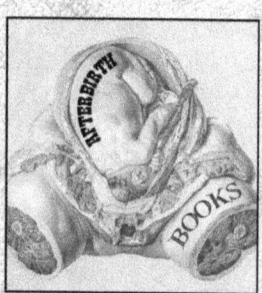

www.afterbirthbooks.com

www.swallowdownpress.com

For all your Bizarro needs visit:

WWW.BIZARROCENTRAL.COM

Introduce yourselves to the bizarro genre and all of its authors with the Bizarro Starter Kit series. Each volume features short novels and short stories by ten of the leading bizarro authors, designed to give you a perfect sampling of the genre for only $5 plus shipping.

BB-0X1
"The Bizarro Starter Kit"
(Orange)

Featuring D. Harlan Wilson, Carlton Mellick III, Jeremy Robert Johnson, Kevin L Donihe, Gina Ranalli, Andre Duza, Vincent W. Sakowski, Steve Beard, John Edward Lawson, and Bruce Taylor.

236 pages $5

BB-0X2
"The Bizarro Starter Kit"
(Blue)

Featuring Ray Fracalossy, Jeremy C. Shipp, Jordan Krall, Mykle Hansen, Andersen Prunty, Eckhard Gerdes, Bradley Sands, Steve Aylett, Christian TeBordo, and Tony Rauch.

244 pages $5

BB-001 "The Kafka Effekt" D. Harlan Wilson - A collection of forty-four irreal short stories loosely written in the vein of Franz Kafka, with more than a pinch of William S. Burroughs sprinkled on top. 211 pages $14

BB-002 "Satan Burger" Carlton Mellick III - The cult novel that put Carlton Mellick III on the map ... Six punks get jobs at a fast food restaurant owned by the devil in a city violently overpopulated by surreal alien cultures. 236 pages $14

BB-003 "Some Things Are Better Left Unplugged" Vincent Sakwoski - Join The Man and his Nemesis, the obese tabby, for a nightmare roller coaster ride into this postmodern fantasy. 152 pages $10

BB-004 "Shall We Gather At the Garden?" Kevin L Donihe - Donihe's Debut novel. Midgets take over the world, The Church of Lionel Richie vs. The Church of the Byrds, plant porn and more! 244 pages $14

BB-005 "Razor Wire Pubic Hair" Carlton Mellick III - A genderless humandildo is purchased by a razor dominatrix and brought into her nightmarish world of bizarre sex and mutilation. 176 pages $11

BB-006 "Stranger on the Loose" D. Harlan Wilson - The fiction of Wilson's 2nd collection is planted in the soil of normalcy, but what grows out of that soil is a dark, witty, otherworldly jungle... 228 pages $14

BB-007 "The Baby Jesus Butt Plug" Carlton Mellick III - Using clones of the Baby Jesus for anal sex will be the hip sex fetish of the future. 92 pages $10

BB-008 "Fishyfleshed" Carlton Mellick III - The world of the past is an illogical flatland lacking in dimension and color, a sick-scape of crispy squid people wandering the desert for no apparent reason. 260 pages $14

BB-009 **"Dead Bitch Army" Andre Duza** - Step into a world filled with racist teenagers, cannibals, 100 warped Uncle Sams, automobiles with razor-sharp teeth, living graffiti, and a pissed-off zombie bitch out for revenge. **344 pages $16**

BB-010 **"The Menstruating Mall" Carlton Mellick III** - "The Breakfast Club meets Chopping Mall as directed by David Lynch." - Brian Keene **212 pages $12**

BB-011 **"Angel Dust Apocalypse" Jeremy Robert Johnson** - Meth-heads, man-made monsters, and murderous Neo-Nazis. "Seriously amazing short stories..." - Chuck Palahniuk, author of Fight Club **184 pages $11**

BB-012 **"Ocean of Lard" Kevin L Donihe / Carlton Mellick III** - A parody of those old Choose Your Own Adventure kid's books about some very odd pirates sailing on a sea made of animal fat. **176 pages $12**

BB-013 **"Last Burn in Hell" John Edward Lawson** - From his lurid angst-affair with a lesbian music diva to his ascendance as unlikely pop icon the one constant for Kenrick Brimley, official state prison gigolo, is he's got no clue what he's doing. **172 pages $14**

BB-014 **"Tangerinephant" Kevin Dole 2** - TV-obsessed aliens have abducted Michael Tangerinephant in this bizarre combination of science fiction, satire, and surrealism. **164 pages $11**

BB-015 **"Foop!" Chris Genoa** - Strange happenings are going on at Dactyl, Inc, the world's first and only time travel tourism company.
"A surreal pie in the face!" - Christopher Moore **300 pages $14**

BB-016 **"Spider Pie" Alyssa Sturgill** - A one-way trip down a rabbit hole inhabited by sexual deviants and friendly monsters, fairytale beginnings and hideous endings. **104 pages $11**

BB-017 "The Unauthorized Woman" Efrem Emerson - Enter the world of the inner freak, a landscape populated by the pre-dead and morticioners, by cockroaches and 300-lb robots. **104 pages $11**

BB-018 "Fugue XXIX" Forrest Aguirre - Tales from the fringe of speculative literary fiction where innovative minds dream up the future's uncharted territories while mining forgotten treasures of the past. **220 pages $16**

BB-019 "Pocket Full of Loose Razorblades" John Edward Lawson - A collection of dark bizarro stories. From a giant rectum to a foot-fungus factory to a girl with a biforked tongue. **190 pages $13**

BB-020 "Punk Land" Carlton Mellick III - In the punk version of Heaven, the anarchist utopia is threatened by corporate fascism and only Goblin, Mortician's sperm, and a blue-mohawked female assassin named Shark Girl can stop them. **284 pages $15**

BB-021 "Pseudo-City" D. Harlan Wilson - Pseudo-City exposes what waits in the bathroom stall, under the manhole cover and in the corporate boardroom, all in a way that can only be described as mind-bogglingly irreal. **220 pages $16**

BB-022 "Kafka's Uncle and Other Strange Tales" Bruce Taylor - Anslenot and his giant tarantula (tormentor? fri-end?) wander a desecrated world in this novel and collection of stories from Mr. Magic Realism Himself. **348 pages $17**

BB-023 "Sex and Death In Television Town" Carlton Mellick III - In the old west, a gang of hermaphrodite gunslingers take refuge from a demon plague in Telos: a town where its citizens have televisions instead of heads. **184 pages $12**

BB-024 "It Came From Below The Belt" Bradley Sands - What can Grover Goldstein do when his severed, sentient penis forces him to return to high school and help it win the presidential election? **204 pages $13**

BB-025 "Sick: An Anthology of Illness" John Lawson, editor - These Sick stories are horrendous and hilarious dissections of creative minds on the scalpel's edge. **296 pages $16**

BB-026 "Tempting Disaster" John Lawson, editor - A shocking and alluring anthology from the fringe that examines our culture's obsession with taboos. **260 pages $16**

BB-027 "Siren Promised" Jeremy Robert Johnson & Alan M Clark - Nominated for the Bram Stoker Award. A potent mix of bad drugs, bad dreams, brutal bad guys, and surreal/incredible art by Alan M. Clark. **190 pages $13**

BB-028 "Chemical Gardens" Gina Ranalli - Ro and punk band Green is the Enemy find Kreepkins, a surfer-dude warlock, a vengeful demon, and a Metal Priestess in their way as they try to escape an underground nightmare. **188 pages $13**

BB-029 "Jesus Freaks" Andre Duza - For God so loved the world that he gave his only two begotten sons... and a few million zombies. **400 pages $16**

BB-030 "Grape City" Kevin L. Donihe - More Donihe-style comedic bizarro about a demon named Charles who is forced to work a minimum wage job on Earth after Hell goes out of business. **108 pages $10**

BB-031 "Sea of the Patchwork Cats" Carlton Mellick III - A quiet dreamlike tale set in the ashes of the human race. For Mellick enthusiasts who also adore The Twilight Zone. **112 pages $10**

BB-032 "Extinction Journals" Jeremy Robert Johnson - An uncanny voyage across a newly nuclear America where one man must confront the problems associated with loneliness, insane dieties, radiation, love, and an ever-evolving cockroach suit with a mind of its own. **104 pages $10**

BB-033 **"Meat Puppet Cabaret" Steve Beard** - At last! The secret connection between Jack the Ripper and Princess Diana's death revealed! **240 pages $16 / $30**

BB-034 **"The Greatest Fucking Moment in Sports" Kevin L. Donihe** - In the tradition of the surreal anti-sitcom Get A Life comes a tale of triumph and agape love from the master of comedic bizarro. **108 pages $10**

BB-035 **"The Troublesome Amputee" John Edward Lawson** - Disturbing verse from a man who truly believes nothing is sacred and intends to prove it. **104 pages $9**

BB-036 **"Deity" Vic Mudd** - God (who doesn't like to be called "God") comes down to a typical, suburban, Ohio family for a little vacation—but it doesn't turn out to be as relaxing as He had hoped it would be... **168 pages $12**

  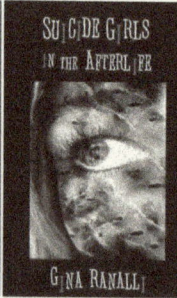 

BB-037 **"The Haunted Vagina" Carlton Mellick III** - It's difficult to love a woman whose vagina is a gateway to the world of the dead. **132 pages $10**

BB-038 **"Tales from the Vinegar Wasteland" Ray Fracalossy** - Witness: a man is slowly losing his face, a neighbor who periodically screams out for no apparent reason, and a house with a room that doesn't actually exist. **240 pages $14**

BB-039 **"Suicide Girls in the Afterlife" Gina Ranalli** - After Pogue commits suicide, she unexpectedly finds herself an unwilling "guest" at a hotel in the Afterlife, where she meets a group of bizarre characters, including a goth Satan, a hippie Jesus, and an alien-human hybrid. **100 pages $9**

BB-040 **"And Your Point Is?" Steve Aylett** - In this follow-up to LINT multiple authors provide critical commentary and essays about Jeff Lint's mind-bending literature. **104 pages $11**

BB-041 **"Not Quite One of the Boys" Vincent Sakowski** - While drug-dealer Maxi drinks with Dante in purgatory, God and Satan play a little tri-level chess and do a little bargaining over his business partner, Vinnie, who is still left on earth. **220 pages $14**

BB-042 **"Teeth and Tongue Landscape" Carlton Mellick III** - On a planet made out of meat, a socially-obsessive monophobic man tries to find his place amongst the strange creatures and communities that he comes across. **110   pages $10**

BB-043 **"War Slut"   Carlton Mellick III** - Part "1984," part "Waiting for Godot," and part action horror video game adaptation of John Carpenter's "The Thing." **116 pages $10**

BB-044 **"All Encompassing Trip"   Nicole Del Sesto** - In a world where coffee is no longer available, the only television shows are reality TV re-runs, and the animals are talking back, Nikki, Amber and a singing Coyote in a do-rag are out to restore the light   **308 pages $15**

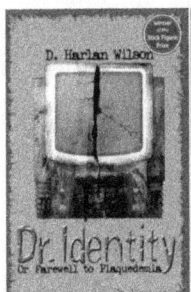   

BB-045 **"Dr. Identity"   D. Harlan Wilson** - Follow the Dystopian Duo on a killing spree of epic proportions through the irreal postcapitalist city of Bliptown where time ticks sideways, artificial Bug-Eyed Monsters punish citizens for consumer-capitalist lethargy, and ultraviolence is as essential as a daily multivitamin. **208 pages $15**

BB-046 **"The Million-Year Centipede"   Eckhard Gerdes** - Wakelin, frontman for 'The Hinge,' wrote a poem so prophetic that to ignore it dooms a person to drown in blood. **130 pages $12**

BB-047 **"Sausagey Santa"   Carlton Mellick III** - A bizarro Christmas tale featuring Santa as a piratey mutant with a body made of sausages. 124 pages $10

BB-048 **"Misadventures in a Thumbnail Universe" Vincent Sakowski** - Dive deep into the surreal and satirical realms of neo-classical Blender Fiction, filled with television shoes and flesh-filled skies. **120 pages $10**

BB-049 **"Vacation" Jeremy C. Shipp** - Blueblood Bernard Johnson leaves his boring life behind to go on The Vacation, a year-long corporate sponsored odyssey. But instead of seeing the world, Bernard is captured by terrorists, becomes a key figure in secret drug wars, and, worse, doesn't once miss his secure American Dream. **160 pages $14**

BB-051 **"13 Thorns" Gina Ranalli** - Thirteen tales of twisted, bizarro horror. **240 pages $13**

BB-050 **"Discouraging at Best" John Edward Lawson** - A collection where the absurdity of the mundane expands exponentially creating a tidal wave that sweeps reason away. For those who enjoy satire, bizarro, or a good old-fashioned slap to the senses. **208 pages $15**

BB-052 **"Better Ways of Being Dead" Christian TeBordo** - In this class, the students have to keep one palm down on the table at all times, and listen to lectures about a panda who speaks Chinese. **216 pages $14**

BB-053 **"Ballad of a Slow Poisoner" Andrew Goldfarb** Millford Mutterwurst sat down on a Tuesday to take his afternoon tea, and made the unpleasant discovery that his elbows were becoming flatter. **128 pages $10**

BB-054 **"Wall of Kiss" Gina Ranalli** - A woman... A wall... Sometimes love blooms in the strangest of places. **108 pages $9**

BB-055 **"HELP! A Bear is Eating Me" Mykle Hansen** - The bizarro, heartwarming, magical tale of poor planning, hubris and severe blood loss...
150 pages $11

BB-056 **"Piecemeal June" Jordan Krall** - A man falls in love with a living sex doll, but with love comes danger when her creator comes after her with crab-squid assassins. **90 pages $9**

BB-057 **"Laredo" Tony Rauch** - Dreamlike, surreal stories by Tony Rauch. **180 pages $12**

BB-058 **"The Overwhelming Urge" Andersen Prunty** - A collection of bizarro tales by Andersen Prunty. **150 pages $11**

BB-059 **"Adolf in Wonderland" Carlton Mellick III** - A dreamlike adventure that takes a young descendant of Adolf Hitler's design and sends him down the rabbit hole into a world of imperfection and disorder. **180 pages $11**

BB-060 **"Super Cell Anemia" Duncan B. Barlow** - "Unrelentingly bizarre and mysterious, unsettling in all the right ways..." - Brian Evenson. **180 pages $12**

BB-061 **"Ultra Fuckers" Carlton Mellick III** - Absurdist suburban horror about a couple who enter an upper middle class gated community but can't find their way out. **108 pages $9**

BB-062 **"House of Houses" Kevin L. Donihe** - An odd man wants to marry his house. Unfortunately, all of the houses in the world collapse at the same time in the Great House Holocaust. Now he must travel to House Heaven to find his departed fiancee. **172 pages $11**

BB-063 **"Necro Sex Machine" Andre Duza** - The Dead Bitch returns in this follow-up to the bizarro zombie epic Dead Bitch Army. **400 pages $16**

BB-064 **"Squid Pulp Blues" Jordan Krall** - In these three bizarro-noir novellas, the reader is thrown into a world of murderers, drugs made from squid parts, deformed gun-toting veterans, and a mischievous apocalyptic donkey. **204 pages $12**

BB-065 "Jack and Mr. Grin" Andersen Prunty - "When Mr. Grin calls you can hear a smile in his voice. Not a warm and friendly smile, but the kind that seizes your spine in fear. You don't need to pay your phone bill to hear it. That smile is in every line of Prunty's prose." - Tom Bradley. **208 pages $12**

BB-066 "Cybernetrix" Carlton Mellick III - What would you do if your normal everyday world was slowly mutating into the video game world from Tron? **212 pages $12**

BB-067 "Lemur" Tom Bradley - Spencer Sproul is a would-be serial-killing bus boy who can't manage to murder, injure, or even scare anybody. However, there are other ways to do damage to far more people and do it legally... **120 pages $12**

BB-068 "Cocoon of Terror" Jason Earls - Decapitated corpses...a sculpture of terror...Zelian's masterpiece, his Cocoon of Terror, will trigger a supernatural disaster for everyone on Earth. **196 pages $14**

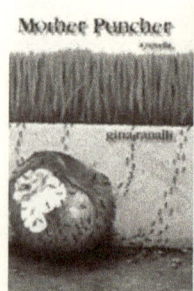 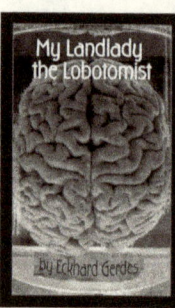  

BB-069 "Mother Puncher" Gina Ranalli - The world has become tragically over-populated and now the government strongly opposes procreation. Ed is employed by the government as a mother-puncher. He doesn't relish his job, but he knows it has to be done and he knows he's the best one to do it. **120 pages $9**

BB-070 "My Landlady the Lobotomist" Eckhard Gerdes - The brains of past tenants line the shelves of my boarding house, soaking in a mysterious elixir. One more slip-up and the landlady might just add my frontal lobe to her collection. **116 pages $12**

BB-071 "CPR for Dummies" Mickey Z. - This hilarious freakshow at the world's end is the fragmented, sobering debut novel by acclaimed nonfiction author Mickey Z. **216 pages $14**

BB-072 "Zerostrata" Andersen Prunty - Hansel Nothing lives in a tree house, suffers from memory loss, has a very eccentric family, and falls in love with a woman who runs naked through the woods every night. **144 pages $11**

BB-073 **"The Egg Man" Carlton Mellick III** - It is a world where humans reproduce like insects. Children are the property of corporations, and having an enormous ten-foot brain implanted into your skull is a grotesque sexual fetish. Mellick's industrial urban dystopia is one of his darkest and grittiest to date. **184 pages $11**

BB-074 **"Shark Hunting in Paradise Garden" Cameron Pierce** - A group of strange humanoid religious fanatics travel back in time to the Garden of Eden to discover it is invested with hundreds of giant flying maneating sharks. **150 pages $10**

BB-075 **"Apeshit" Carlton Mellick III** - Friday the 13th meets Visitor Q. Six hipster teens go to a cabin in the woods inhabited by a deformed killer. An incredibly fucked-up parody of B-horror movies with a bizarro slant. **192 pages $12**

BB-076 **"Rampaging Fuckers of Everything on the Crazy Shitting Planet of the Vomit At smosphere" Mykle Hansen** - 3 bizarro satires. Monster Cocks, Journey to the Center of Agnes Cuddlebottom, and Crazy Shitting Planet. **228 pages $12**

BB-077 **"The Kissing Bug" Daniel Scott Buck** - In the tradition of Roald Dahl, Tim Burton, and Edward Gorey, comes this bizarro anti-war children's story about a bohemian conenose kissing bug who falls in love with a human woman. **116 pages $10**

BB-078 **"MachoPoni" Lotus Rose** - It's My Little Pony... *Bizarro* style! A long time ago Poniworld was split in two. On one side of the Jagged Line is the Pastel Kingdom, a magical land of music, parties, and positivity. On the other side of the Jagged Line is Dark Kingdom inhabited by an army of undead ponies. **148 pages $11**

BB-079 **"The Faggiest Vampire" Carlton Mellick III** - A Roald Dahl-esque children's story about two faggy vampires who partake in a mustache competition to find out which one is truly the faggiest. **104 pages $10**

BB-080 **"Sky Tongues" Gina Ranalli** - The autobiography of Sky Tongues, the biracial hermaphrodite actress with tongues for fingers. Follow her strange life story as she rises from freak to fame. **204 pages $12**

BB-081 "Washer Mouth" Kevin L. Donihe - A washing machine becomes human and pursues his dream of meeting his favorite soap opera star. **244 pages $11**

BB-082 "Shatnerquake" Jeff Burk - All of the characters ever played by William Shatner are suddenly sucked into our world. Their mission: hunt down and destroy the real William Shatner. **100 pages $10**

BB-083 "The Cannibals of Candyland" Carlton Mellick III - There exists a race of cannibals that are made of candy. They live in an underground world made out of candy. One man has dedicated his life to killing them all. **170 pages $11**

BB-084 "Slub Glub in the Weird World of the Weeping Willows" Andrew Goldfarb - The charming tale of a blue glob named Slub Glub who helps the weeping willows whose tears are flooding the earth. There are also hyenas, ghosts, and a voodoo priest **100 pages $10**

BB-085 "Super Fetus" Adam Pepper - Try to abort this fetus and he'll kick your ass! **104 pages $10**

BB-086 "Fistful of Feet" Jordan Krall - A bizarro tribute to spaghetti westerns, featuring Cthulhu-worshipping Indians, a woman with four feet, a crazed gunman who is obsessed with sucking on candy, Syphilis-ridden mutants, sexually transmitted tattoos, and a house devoted to the freakiest fetishes. **228 pages $12**

BB-087 "Ass Goblins of Auschwitz" Cameron Pierce - It's Monty Python meets Nazi exploitation in a surreal nightmare as can only be imagined by Bizarro author Cameron Pierce. **104 pages $10**

BB-088 "Silent Weapons for Quiet Wars" Cody Goodfellow - "This is high-end psychological surrealist horror meets bottom-feeding low-life crime in a techno-thrilling science fiction world full of Lovecraft and magic..." -John Skipp **212 pages $12**

BB-089 "Warrior Wolf Women of the Wasteland" Carlton Mellick III - Road Warrior Werewolves versus McDonaldland Mutants...post-apocalyptic fiction has never been quite like this. **316 pages $13**

BB-090 "Cursed" Jeremy C Shipp - The story of a group of characters who believe they are cursed and attempt to figure out who cursed them and why. A tale of stylish absurdism and suspenseful horror. **218 pages $15**

BB-091 "Super Giant Monster Time" Jeff Burk - A tribute to choose your own adventures and Godzilla movies. Will you escape the giant monsters that are rampaging the fuck out of your city and shit? Or will you join the mob of alien-controlled punk rockers causing chaos in the streets? What happens next depends on you. **188 pages $12**

BB-092 "Perfect Union" Cody Goodfellow - "Cronenberg's THE FLY on a grand scale: human/insect gene-spliced body horror, where the human hive politics are as shocking as the gore." -John Skipp. **272 pages $13**

BB-093 "Sunset with a Beard" Carlton Mellick III - 14 stories of surreal science fiction. **200 pages $12**

BB-094 "My Fake War" Andersen Prunty - The absurd tale of an unlikely soldier forced to fight a war that, quite possibly, does not exist. It's Rambo meets Waiting for Godot in this subversive satire of American values and the scope of the human imagination. **128 pages $11**

BB-095 "Lost in Cat Brain Land" Cameron Pierce - Sad stories from a surreal world. A fascist mustache, the ghost of Franz Kafka, a desert inside a dead cat. Primordial entities mourn the death of their child. The desperate serve tea to mysterious creatures. A hopeless romantic falls in love with a pterodactyl. And much more. **152 pages $11**

BB-096 "The Kobold Wizard's Dildo of Enlightenment +2" Carlton Mellick III - A Dungeons and Dragons parody about a group of people who learn they are only made up characters in an AD&D campaign and must find a way to resist their nerdy teenaged players and retarded dungeon master in order to survive. **232 pages $12**

BB-097 **"My Heart Said No, but the Camera Crew Said Yes!" Bradley Sands** - A collection of short stories that are crammed with the delightfully odd and the scurrilously silly. **140 pages $13**

BB-098 **"A Hundred Horrible Sorrows of Ogner Stump" Andrew Goldfarb** - Goldfarb's acclaimed comic series. A magical and weird journey into the horrors of everyday life. **164 pages $11**

BB-099 **"Pickled Apocalypse of Pancake Island" Cameron Pierce** A demented fairy tale about a pickle, a pancake, and the apocalypse. **102 pages $8**

BB-100 **"Slag Attack" Andersen Prunty** - Slag Attack features four visceral, noir stories about the living, crawling apocalypse. A slag is what survivors are calling the slug-like maggots raining from the sky, burrowing inside people, and hollowing out their flesh and their sanity. **148 pages $11**

BB-101 **"Slaughterhouse High" Robert Devereaux** - A place where schools are built with secret passageways, rebellious teens get zippers installed in their mouths and genitals, and once a year, on that special night, one couple is slaughtered and the bits of their bodies are kept as souvenirs. **304 pages $13**

BB-102 **"The Emerald Burrito of Oz" John Skipp & Marc Levinthal** OZ IS REAL! Magic is real! The gate is really in Kansas! And America is finally allowing Earth tourists to visit this weird-ass, mysterious land. But when Gene of Los Angeles heads off for summer vacation in the Emerald City, little does he know that a war is brewing...a war that could destroy both worlds. **280 pages $13**

BB-103 **"The Vegan Revolution... with Zombies" David Agranoff** When there's no more meat in hell, the vegans will walk the earth. **160 pages $11**

BB-104 **"The Flappy Parts" Kevin L Donihe** - Poems about bunnies, LSD, and police abuse. You know, things that matter. **132 pages $11**

ORDER FORM

TITLES	QTY	PRICE	TOTAL

Please make checks and moneyorders payable to ROSE O'KEEFE / BIZARRO BOOKS in U.S. funds only. Please don't send bad checks! Allow 2-6 weeks for delivery. International orders may take longer. If you'd like to pay online via PAYPAL.COM, send payments to publisher@eraserheadpress.com.

SHIPPING: US ORDERS - $2 for the first book, $1 for each additional book. For priority shipping, add an additional $4. INT'L ORDERS - $5 for the first book, $3 for each additional book. Add an additional $5 per book for global priority shipping.

Send payment to:

BIZARRO BOOKS
C/O Rose O'Keefe
205 NE Bryant
Portland, OR 97211

Address	
City	State Zip
Email	Phone

www.ingramcontent.com/pod-product-compliance
Lightning Source LLC
Chambersburg PA
CBHW032120090426
42743CB00007B/416